Modest Proposals

or May I Call You Mine?

Also by Rosalind Miles

DANGER! MEN AT WORK

ROSALIND MILES

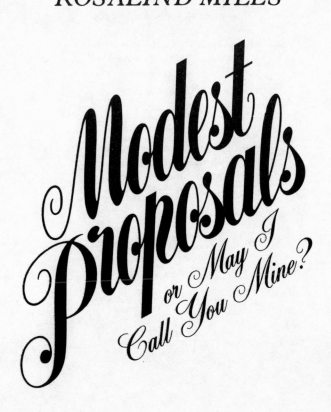

Modest Proposals
or May I Call You Mine?

MACDONALD & CO
LONDON & SYDNEY

A Macdonald Book

Copyright © Rosalind Miles 1984

First published in Great Britain in 1984
by Macdonald & Co (Publishers) Ltd
London & Sydney
A BPCC plc Company

ISBN 0 356 10073 1

Typeset, printed and bound in Great Britain by
Hazell Watson & Viney Limited,
Member of the BPCC Group,
Aylesbury, Bucks

419

Macdonald & Co
London & Sydney
Maxwell House
74 Worship Street
London EC2A 2EN

Acknowledgements

The author and publisher would like to thank the following for permission to include copyright material:
Laurence Pollinger Ltd and the Estate of Mrs Frieda Lawrence Ravagli for extracts from *Lady Chatterley's Lover* and *To Women, As Far As I'm Concerned* and *Gipsy* from *The Complete Poems of D. H. Lawrence*; Michael Joseph Ltd, John Farquharson Ltd and the author for an extract from *A Kind of Loving* by Stan Barstow; Martin, Secker & Warburg Ltd and the author for an extract from *Fear of Flying* by Erica Jong; Lady Ethel Wodehouse and Hutchinson Books Limited for extracts from *Damsel in Distress* by P. G. Wodehouse; George Weidenfeld & Nicolson Ltd and the author for extracts from *Scruples* by Judith Krantz; Rupert Crew Ltd and the author for extracts from *The Ruthless Rake* by Barbara Cartland; The National Trust for an extract from *The Female of the Species* by Rudyard Kipling; Macdonald & Co (Publishers) Ltd and the author for extracts from *The Thornbirds* by Colleen McCullough; John Murray and the author for extracts from *Bonjour Tristesse* by Françoise Sagan; Simon & Schuster Inc. and the author for extract from *Marty* from *Television Plays* by Paddy Chayefsky, copyright © 1955 by Paddy Chayefsky, reprinted by permission of Simon & Schuster Inc.; W. H. Allen & Co Ltd and the author for extracts from *Past Imperfect* by Joan Collins; Penguin Books Ltd for an extract from *The Matchmaker* by Thornton Wilder; the Bodley Head for extracts from *The Beautiful and The Damned*, *The Sensible Thing*, *This Side of Paradise* and *The Great Gatsby* by F. Scott Fitzgerald; Corgi Books Ltd, the author and editor for extracts from *Electronic Baby* by Richard

Sylvester taken from *Love, Love, Love* ed. Peter Roche copyright © by Richard Sylvester and reproduced here by permission of Corgi Books Ltd; Plangent Visions Music Limited for *Tunnel of Love* by Fun Boy Three copyright © 1982 reproduced by kind permission of Plangent Visions Music Limited; the Daisy Ashford Literary Estate and Chatto & Windus for extract from *The Young Visitors* by Daisy Ashford; Webb & Bower (Publishers) Ltd and the editor for extracts from *Sweethearts & Valentines* ed. Judith Holder; Northern Songs Limited, 19 Upper Brook St, London for an extract from *When I'm 64* by The Beatles; Faber and Faber Publishers for extracts from *Les Sylphides* from *The Collected Poems of Louis MacNeice* and *The Bell Jar* by Sylvia Plath; Faber and Faber Publishers for an extract from *Johnny* from *The English Auden: Poems, Essays and Dramatic Writings 1927–39* by W. H. Auden and Random House, Inc. and the editor for an extract from *Johnny* from *W. H. Auden Collected Poems* edited by Edward Mendelson; Methuen London for extracts from *Loot* by Joe Orton and *The Hostage* by Brendan Behan; for *Some Enchanted Evening* by Rodgers and Hammerstein, copyright 1949 Richard Rodgers and Oscar Hammerstein II Williamson Music Inc. UK Publisher Williamson Music. Used by permission; Random House Inc. and Jonathan Cape for extracts from *By Myself* by Lauren Bacall and *Portnoy's Complaint* by Philip Roth; the Executors of the Eugene O'Neill Estate and Random House Inc. for extracts from *The Hairy Ape* from *The Plays of Eugene O'Neill*; The extracts from *Hobson's Choice* by Harold Brighouse are reproduced by kind permission of the Estate of Harold Brighouse and Samuel French Ltd; passages from *Memoirs of a Mangy Lover* by Groucho Marx excerpted with the permission of Bernard Geis Associates from *Memoirs of a Mangy Lover* by Groucho Marx © 1963 by Groucho Marx; and excerpts from *Rebecca* with kind permission from Daphne du Maurier.

While every effort has been made to trace copyright holders and obtain permission to use various extracts, this has in some cases proved impossible and the publishers and author would be happy to hear from anyone not here acknowledged.

When two fond hearts
As one unite,
The yoke is easy
And the burden light.

This little poem was the first piece of proposal literature I ever collected. It is inscribed in sepia scrolls and flourishes, surrounded with a riot of hearts and flowers, on a plate that I rushed out and bought in a junk shop the day after I got engaged. If my newly-betrothed thought the plate was not the only thing that was cracked, he had the decency not to say so. And that was the start of my fascination with the whole subject.

So here for your delight as well as mine is a gathering of marriage proposals from the best that has been thought and said over the last five hundred years — the good, the bad, the sad, the funny, the unfulfilled, and the 'Why ever did they bother?' And since not everyone has the same kind of partnership in mind, here too are the manoeuvres of those trying for an unofficial marriage. The result is just what a bride is traditionally supposed to carry on her wedding day, something old, something new, something borrowed and something blue.

Modest Proposals

But I hope that lovers everywhere will find something in here to please or amuse themselves and their best beloved. I would like to thank all those who have helped me with offering material or memories, but especially Mark Lucas; this book comes as a wedding present to you and Melinda, and with it my wish for all the joy in the world for you both. And finally, to any couple who are just on the brink of life's greatest adventure — happy landings!

Rosalind Miles

For
handsome K. M.
lover and friend –
who proposed to me

Contents

I
Modest Proposals

II
Immodest Proposals

III
The Real Thing

I

Modest Proposals

The Immortal Moment

> GARBO: . . . *Wait, wait . . . what's the hurry? Let us be happy . . . give us our moment . . . we are happy, aren't we, Leon?*
> LEON: *(adoringly) Yes, sweetheart. (He folds her in his arms)*
> GARBO: *So happy . . .*
>
> *Ninotchka*

'WILL YOU MARRY ME?' – 'YES!' In this simple question and answer lies the highest expression of human love. This is the moment when the deepest feelings are declared, and lovers claim their full rights in one another. It's the moment when you roll up the map of your future and send it back to be redrawn, the moment of piercing joy when you know that your dearest friend wants to go forward with you and be at your side *always*.

The celebration of this special event has resulted in some of the richest episodes in life and literature. With a proposal of marriage, lovers stand at a crossroads of their lives. Backwards they can see all the chances and episodes that have led them here – forward lie all the adventures that they will share together as a couple. This sense of the past and the future intersecting makes the proposal a unique occasion, a moment out of time, outside time.

Garbo speaks for all lovers when she says, 'give us our moment'. As the world is turned upside down and the powerful feelings of love and joy come thronging in, everyone needs that still, perfect occasion when their two hearts become one in a memory that will live for ever. So what is the ideal proposal? How can the offer of marriage be made worthy of being cherished in loving thoughts, wrapped up in mental cotton-wool for the years ahead?

Maxim de Winter, the hero of Daphne du Maurier's *Rebecca*, thinks he knows. After making a superbly romantic proposal to the heroine, he intensifies the romance of it all by asking her:

> *This isn't at all your idea of a proposal, is it? It should be in a conservatory, you in a white frock with a red rose in your hand and a violin playing in the distance, and I should be making violent love to you behind a palm tree — poor darling, never mind.*

She doesn't, of course. But this version must be quite close to the ideal, since exactly the same themes come up in other proposals. Louis MacNeice in *Les Sylphides* takes his girl to the ballet, where his feelings blend in with the exquisite grace of the dancers:

> *Now, he thought, we are floating — ageless, oarless —*
> *Now there is no separation from now on*
> > *You will be wearing white*
> > *Satin and a red sash*
> > *Under the waltzing trees*

Is this how we'd all like it to be, floating in joy yet frozen in the experience of discovering it, like the lovers on Keats's Grecian urn?

♡ 4 ♡

When the time, the place and the people are right, nothing can prevent the marriage moment from achieving its rightful immortality. H. G. Wells leads his hero, Kipps, through a series of adventures, but none so glorious as his proposal to the lovely Helen. They have climbed to the top of an old castle in Kent, and here, 'high out of the world of every day and in the presence of spacious beauty', Kipps rises to the occasion he has been longing for:

> *'You will marry me?'*
> *'Yes,' she laughed, and 'Yes.'*
> *All the world that evening was no more than a shadowy frame of darkling sky and water and dripping boughs about Helen. He seemed to see through things with an extraordinary clearness; she was revealed to him certainly, as the cause and essence of it all. He was indeed at his Heart's Desire. It was one of those times when there seems to be no future, when time has stopped and we are at the end. Kipps, that evening, could not have imagined a tomorrow — all that his imagination had pointed towards was attained. His mind stood still, and took the moments as they came.*

Like the romantic that he is, Kipps has unconsciously chosen an ideal setting for his proposal. The old castle, the woodland and the river by night all lend their magic to the occasion. But the ravishing natural backdrop is not an essential requirement. When the time is right it can come anywhere, and both lovers will recognize and rise to the destiny that is to make them partners in the fullest sense.

In the most intense experience of coming together, true lovers can even dispense with words to plight their troth. Scott Fitzgerald shows his genius as the world's leading *romancier* when he gives us the moment without the words at the engagement of two of his Jazz Age lovers in *The Beautiful and Damned*:

> *But oh, Anthony's face as he walked down the tenth-floor corridor of the Plaza that night! His dark eyes were gleaming — around his mouth were lines it was a kindness to see. He was handsome then if never before, bound for one of those immortal moments which come so radiantly that their remembered light is enough to see by for years. He knocked, and at a word, entered. Gloria, dressed in simple pink, starched and fresh as a flower, was across the room, standing very still, and looking at him wide-eyed.*
>
> *As he closed the door behind him, she gave a little cry, and moved swiftly over the intervening space, her arms rising in a premature caress as she came near. Together they crushed out the stiff folds of her dress in one triumphant and enduring embrace.*

'. . . one of those immortal moments whose light is enough to see by for years' — that is the ideal of the proposal, so that in time to come the shadow of a smile, the memory of a body, a melody or a scent on the breeze are enough to recall that unique and life-changing emotional climax.

For a marriage proposal is both an end and a beginning. It's both a blinding flash of illumination and the recognition of something obvious that has been there all along, all your life as it seems, the need for the other person. All this in one moment — no wonder that it has been so written about, so treasured up. It's something no one would want to forget. As the heroine says, in *Rebecca* again,

> *. . . there should be an invention that bottles up a memory like a perfume, and it never faded, never got stale, and whenever I wanted to I could uncork the bottle, and live the memory all over again . . .*

The Hope And The Promise

> *Wilt thou be true and just,*
> *And clean and kind and brave?*
>
> A. E. Housman

A MARRIAGE PROPOSAL is a special, sacred moment. But like all beautiful things it has an intricacy which is not immediately apparent. It is, in fact, not so much one moment as a series of moments, one inside another like Chinese boxes, each one giving on to all the others until the very last.

For inside the simple question, 'Will you be mine?' there are a thousand other questions for the man and the woman alike. Will you, can you, they ask silently, be to me all that this most special relationship implies? *Can* we love, comfort, honour and keep one another, forsaking all other, from this day forward, for better for worse, for richer for poorer, in sickness and in health, till death us do part? However much you might be in love, this is still a daunting list of requirements. American couples who make up their own marriage services often leave out the nasty bits. As Bertrand Russell said of the Ten Commandments, there should be a further instruction, 'only six to be attempted'.

Yet it is in the hope of being worthy of this great

undertaking that people want to make the ultimate commitment. The proposal and acceptance of marriage are the lovers' way of showing that they have reached the culmination of life's greatest adventure. They have come to the end of the search for the other half of their soul.

Many songs and stories have celebrated the unique closeness of married partners. Husband and wife can enjoy a sweetness and security unknown to the fevered band of Bed-hoppers Anonymous. As a famous and beautiful actress, Mrs Patrick Campbell had more than her share of the compulsion of the casting couch. She knew what she was talking about when she hailed with relief: *'the deep, deep peace of the double bed after the hurly-burly of the chaise longue'*.

Marriage is, after all, meant to be enjoyed. It's not illegal or immoral, it doesn't make you fat, and the Surgeon General has not yet determined that it is harmful to your health. It could even be good amid the trials and tribulations of founding the New World, according to one of the pioneer women. Anne Bradstreet, America's earliest woman writer, paid this tribute in about 1640 to her partner in married love:

To My Husband

If ever two were one, then surely we;
  If ever man were loved by wife, then thee.
If ever wife were happy in a man,
  Compare with me, ye women, if you can . . .
Thy love is such I no way can repay;
  The heavens reward thee manifold, I pray,
That while we live, in love let's so persever,
  That when we live no more, we may live ever.

Mistress Anne and her husband had a long and happy marriage. And that, after all, is what we're all hoping for

♡ 8 ♡

at the moment of the betrothal. We don't like to think that our marriage is just the first step on the road to the Divorce Courts!

So important is the *unspoken* question – not just 'shall we be married?' but also 'shall we make each other happy?' – that writers will often glance forward from the proposal into the future to answer it. One faithful soul who fully deserves the reward of happiness in marriage is Dobbin in Thackeray's *Vanity Fair*. He has loved Amelia long and hopelessly all his life. Eventually concluding that his love will never prosper, he goes away.

Dobbin's departure brings Amelia to her senses. Although shy and frail, she is not too timid to call him back to her side. As Dobbin is the quintessential English-man, his great moment occurs appropriately enough in a downpour of rain. But even all the waters of the sea are not enough to quench the ardour of the reunion as his ship comes in:

> *As the gentleman in the old cloak lined with red stuff stepped on to the shore, there was scarcely any one present to see what took place, which was briefly, this –*
>
> *A lady in a dripping white bonnet and shawl, with her two little hands out before her, went up to him, and in the next minute she had altogether disappeared under the folds of the old cloak, and was kissing one of his hands with all her might; whilst the other, I suppose, was engaged in holding her to his heart (which her head just about reached) and in preventing her from tumbling down. She was murmuring something about – forgive – dear William – dear, dear, dearest friend – kiss, kiss, kiss, and so forth – in fact went on under the cloak in an absurd manner . . .*
>
> *'It was time you sent for me, dear Amelia,' he said.*
>
> *'You will never go again, William?'*

♡ 9 ♡

> *'No, never,' he answered, and pressed the dear little soul once more to his heart.*

Dobbin has suffered enormously while waiting for this. But now his time has come:

> *The vessel is in port. He has got the prize he has been trying for all his life. The bird has come in at last. There it is with its head on his shoulder, billing and cooing close up to his heart, with soft outstretched fluttering wings. This is what he has asked for every day and hour for eighteen years. This is what he pined after . . . God bless you, William! – farewell, dear Amelia. Grow green again, tender little plant, round the rugged oak to which you cling!*

Every proposal of marriage asks for a once and future love. It's an expression of hope that the hands which are joined today will link even more strongly as time goes by. Its acceptance is a silent answer to the Beatles' jokey question:

> *When I get older, losing my hair,*
> *Many years from now,*
> *Will you still be sending me a Valentine,*
> *Birthday greetings, bottle of wine,*
> *If I'd been out till quarter to three,*
> *Would you lock the door,*
> *Will you still need me, will you still feed me,*
> *When I'm sixty-four?*

As the song warns, 'you'll be older too'. But when a married couple are really travelling together, getting older becomes just one of the experiences which bring them closer. When two people succeed in making something lasting, the passage of time will only ripen and enrich the bouquet. And it must be nice to have someone around who remembers you before you had your false teeth, glasses and hearing aid!

Of course there's no one like a reformed rake for extolling the joys of wedlock. Nobody who knew Robbie Burns in his roving days would ever have believed that he would settle down to being one of the folks that live on the hill. Yet this gallant of the glens, from whom no girl in the whole of Scotland was safe, wrote one of the warmest songs of married love. In the last verse, the wife looks back with mischievous glee on their life together, and forward with complete serenity to the final parting of their ways:

> *John Anderson, my jo, John,*
> *We climbed the hill together,*
> *And many a canty day, John,*
> *We've had with one another.*
> *Now we maun totter down,*
> *John,*
> *And hand-in-hand we'll go,*
> *And sleep together at the foot,*
> *John Anderson, my jo.*

There's something very attractive about a Scot, whether Sir Walter, the heroic Captain, or Randolph C. Maybe that's why Robert Burns is top of the pops in the Soviet Union — they can't have many writers as 'canty' as he is. His famous numbers like 'My Love Is Like A Red Red Rose' sound even better, if possible, in Russian than in Scots. And wherever in the world a couple are together enjoying their marriage, 'John Anderson' cannot fail to strike a chord.

But of all the marriage proposals which catch up the future in the moment of sealing the bond, the most powerful comes at the climax of George Eliot's *Adam Bede*. Adam is passionately in love with Dinah, a deeply religious girl who feels that she must devote her life to helping others. As she is about to go away to begin this work, Adam cannot help himself asking her not to go but to 'stay and be my dear wife'.

To his joy, Dinah confesses her love for Adam: 'My heart waits on your words and looks almost like a little child . . .' But she is afraid that this is only a temptation to turn her from her path, and asks for time to consider. At last Adam goes to hear her answer:

> *What a look of yearning love it was that the mild grey eyes turned on the strong dark-eyed man! She said nothing, but moved towards him so that his arm could clasp her round.*
>
> *And they walked on so in silence while the warm tears fell. 'Adam,' she said, 'it is the Divine will. My soul is so knit to yours that it is but a divided life I live without you. And this moment, now you are with me, and I feel that our hearts are filled with the same love, I have a fullness of strength to bear and do our Heavenly Father's will, that I had lost before.'*
>
> *Adam paused, and looked into her sincere and loving eyes.*
>
> *'Then we'll never part any more, Dinah, till death parts us.'*
>
> *And they kissed each other with deep joy.*
>
> *What greater thing is there for two human souls than to feel that they are joined for life — to strengthen each other in all labour, to rest on each other in all sorrow, to minister to each other in all pain, to be one with each other in silent, unspeakable memories at the moment of the last parting?*

What indeed? And may every couple embarking on the hope and the promise of marriage together be spared to enjoy this kindness of fate!

♡ 12 ♡

3

The Forces Against

> *'You got to get married,' said Uncle Penstemon.*
> *'That's the way of it. I done it long before I was your*
> *age. It's nat'ral — like poaching, or drinking, or wind*
> *on the stummik. You can't 'elp it, and there you are!'*

H. G. Wells, *The History of Mr Polly*

THE IDEAL PROPOSAL is a magical moment, a peak of ecstasy amid a whirl of impression of beauty — ballgowns and roses, passion and palm trees, with the strains of heavenly music wafting in the distance. But many people's experience falls far short of this ideal — they get the strains without the music.

Alida Baxter, for instance, found that her marriage proposal could hardly have occurred at a less propitious time and place. As she ruefully confesses in her autobiography, *Flat On My Back*:

> *I wouldn't be married at all if it weren't for that stomach*
> *upset I had in 1969. I was run down, and being proposed*
> *to through the lavatory door caught me off guard.*

Yes, well, it would, wouldn't it? In fairness the Baxter swain had been doing sterling work nursing his inamorata through a combination of Montezuma's Revenge and the

Black Death, on what was supposed to be a jolly holiday in Spain. When language broke down with the Mediterranean medico, he even carried devotion to the extent of *miming* her complaint for the doctor's better understanding – which was, in fact, diarrhoea!

Now a man who'll mime diarrhoea for you in front of a grinning foreigner is clearly a man of many parts, but a sense of timing was not among them. He waited until his true love was philosophizing from the depths of the bathroom about the division of the Spanish nation into sadists and masochists – 'the sadists manufacture the toilet paper, and the masochists use it' – and chose this tender moment to pop the question. As she says herself:

> *There can't be all that many people who've received a proposal of marriage through a lavatory door and I sometimes consider ringing up the* Guinness Book Of Records, *but perhaps an ex-nurse friend of mine has the edge on me. Her husband proposed to her after she'd given him an enema.*

Ah. Yes, well, could have been worse, then! But either way, one of the obstacles to a proper proposal is the lack of a sense of romance. To some, marriage is not an emotional adventure, but a dragging social duty. This is how it strikes the writer Michaelis in D. H. Lawrence's *Lady Chatterley's Lover.* He is, on his own admission, a lonely bird, but he has no hope that his loneliness would be relieved by marriage:

> *'I'm thirty . . . yes, I'm thirty!' said Michaelis sharply and suddenly, '. . . and I'm going to marry. Oh yes, I must marry.'*
> *'It sounds like going to have your tonsils out,' laughed Connie. 'Will it be an effort?'*

'Well, Lady Chatterley, somehow it will!'

You can just imagine from this the sort of woman he will choose, a beak-faced harpy who will make proposing feel like having your tonsils taken out, without anaesthetic. Some men simply are not the stuff that a good proposer is made of. Groucho Marx just can't see the reason for it all, as he explains in his *Memoirs Of A Mangy Lover*:

> *Personally, I don't see why a man can't have a dog AND a girl. But if you can afford only one, get a dog. For example, if your dog sees you playing with another dog, does he rush to his lawyer and bark that your marriage is on the rocks and that he wants 600 bones a month alimony, the good car, and the little forty-thousand-dollar home that still has a nineteen-thousand-dollar mortgage on it?*

Even when the man is up to the mark, obstacles may bar his way. Every budding couple needs peace and privacy to get things sorted out on their own. But in the history of courtship and proposal, families are all too often determined that this is the last thing they should have. That's why all the really great lovers of history and legend, from Antony and Cleopatra to Hepburn and Tracy, have nobody but themselves on the scene. They are alone together in their own private world. Having a family can have the direst possible consequences for lovers – witness Shakespeare's *Romeo and Juliet*.

The greater the family, the greater the capacity for interference. When Lord Randolph Churchill fell in love with Miss Jennie Jerome in 1873, the family did its utmost to strangle marriage plans at birth. She was, after all, American, and her father was in business. These twin handicaps meant that she was far more likely to be shown the tradesman's entrance of a great English ducal house, than be allowed to marry into it.

The parents were content to play a waiting game. But Randolph's elder brother had himself made a bitterly unhappy marriage, which in his view made him an expert on the subject. He came down on Randolph like a ton of bricks, in a letter positively pulsating with rage:

Consider once more! Risk anything! BUT DON'T MARRY! I tell you that you are mad simply mad. I don't care if la demoiselle was the incarnation of all moral excellencies and physical beauties on God's earth . . . marriage is a delusion and a snare like all the rest, only with this disagreeable addition that it is irrevocable.

Have you any solid end in view in this affair? No!

Do you marry for a fortune? No!

Do you marry to get children? No!

Do you marry because you have loved a woman for years? No!

Do you marry because you are getting old and played out? No!

You really only want to marry because you are in love with an idea. DAMNATION! My dear Randolph for God's sake listen to me . . .

Amazingly, Lord Randolph stood firm under this battery, and went on to repeat his proposal to Jennie Jerome in form. She married him, and subsequently became the mother of Winston Churchill. What more could any woman have done for England?

But Jennie's life was to be dogged by domineering males poking their noses into her love affairs. Later, after she was widowed, she was courted by a much younger man. No less a person than Edward, Prince of Wales, intervened this time, to tell her that if she married her lover she would never be able to mix in court circles again. This was a royal act of humbug from the princely hypocrite, to condone an *affair* but not a *marriage* – and the Prince's own dedication to the art of the horizontal hardly qualified him to give a moral lead! In the end Jennie cocked the aristocratic equivalent of two fingers at the whole pack of them, married her lover anyway, and did not lose either her friends or her position.

In the past the real threat came not from outsiders but in the person of the girl's father. He was, after all, for many years the actual owner of his daughter in the eyes of the law. She was his chattel to dispose of as he pleased. The true situation of a girl under this system is sharply highlighted by Shakespeare in the brutal outburst of Juliet's father when she refuses to marry the man of his choice:

> *If you be mine, I'll give you to my friend;*
> *If you be not, hang, beg, starve, die in the streets!*

Fortunately, most fathers do not take their disapproval of their daughters' suitors quite so much to heart. Nevertheless they can still give young hopefuls a rough time. The qualities likely to make a girl fall in love with you can be the very opposite of those designed to appeal to her father, as Robert Browning found out when he courted Miss Elizabeth Barrett of Wimpole Street. The father, with his ex-officio power of veto, has to be won over, placated, or somehow neutralized.

Consequently, going to ask a father for his daughter's hand in marriage was an even greater trial than securing the aforementioned mitt in the first place. Strindberg gives a humorous account of the process, thought to be based on his own experience, in *Getting Married*:

When he went to see the major to propose, the notary had not looked up the quotations for grain, but the major had.

'I love her,' said the notary.

'How much do you earn?' asked the old gentleman.

'Only twelve hundred crowns I know, but we love each other, sir . . .'

'I'm not interested, twelve hundred's too little.'

'I earn a bit more than that in fact, but Louise knows the ardour of my heart . . .'

'Don't talk nonsense, how much do you earn?' His pen was poised ready to write.

'And what about her feelings, sir? Do you know how . . .?'

'Will you give me an answer, sir, or won't you! How much more do you earn? Figures, sir! Figures. Facts!'

'I do translations at ten crowns the quire. I give lessons in French. I've been promised proof-reading.'

'At ten crowns a quire. Comes to 250 crowns and then what?'

And then what? Under this harassment the young man, probably sweating like a horse by this time, begins to crack up:

'Then? I never know in advance.'

'That's just it! You don't know in advance. But that's just what you must do. You think that getting married is merely a matter of moving in together and making fools of yourselves. No, my boy, there'll be a child in nine months' time, and a child needs food and clothing.'

'There needn't be a child straight away. When two people love each other as we do, sir, as we do . . .'

'How the devil do you love each other, then?'

'Do you think I can put our love into words?' placing his hand on the lapel of his waistcoat.

♡ 18 ♡

> *'And you think there won't be a child when you love like that? Idiot! You're a damned idiot, sir! However, they say you're a decent sort of fellow, so I'll let you get engaged. But mind you spend the time of your engagement on bread-winning, for there are hard times ahead. GRAIN IS GOING UP!'*

This sounds like a pretty rough ride for a would-be husband. But it is, in fact, par for the course. Nineteenth-century fathers used to seize with relish the chance to tyrannize over prospective sons-in-law, and shamelessly add to the anguish of mind the poor chaps were going through at this climax of their lives anyway!

Modern men have no idea of their good luck in being able to bypass this excruciating ritual. Some, of course, still have to do it. HRH Prince Charles did Earl Spencer the honour of asking for Lady Diana's hand, eyes, shy smile etc. But he must have felt pretty confident that the Earl was not about to turn purple in the face, call him a bounder and a cad, grab the nearest shotgun and chase him off the ancestral acres. Among lesser mortals the future-father-in-law routine has become so disused that one recently-betrothed suitor found that though he'd been up all night writing the script, so to speak, the old boy didn't know his words, refused to play his part, and the whole scene was over in forty-five seconds!

As this shows, some fathers would just as happily *not* be asked. This is particularly true for a father of many daughters, who can gloomily foresee it coming again and again. The chap who proposed to my eldest sister one Saturday night could not wait to get the man-to-man business over and done with. He presented himself at the house in his best suit, exuding aftershave and nervous tension from every pore, at ten to eight on the following Sunday morning.

But the other man was not quite so keen. The *pater familias* was in fact detected trying to leave the house surreptitiously by the back door, still in his dressing gown and slippers. By the time he had been hotly pursued, apprehended, scolded rotten and turned into the sitting room to meet his fate, the future son-in-law was on the point of expiry. Listening outside the door, all the females heard the scene proceed in a series of blurts, gasps, and nervous tics. Afterwards Pa made just one proviso — that he should be allowed to receive all future requests for his daughters' hands with his trousers on, and preferably with a glass in his hand!

But of all prospective fathers-in-law, the most sorely tried must have been the father of Olivia Langdon, the best beloved of Samuel Clemens ('Mark Twain'). Clemens was a great admirer of women and by common consent at his best in their company: 'he loved the minds of women, their wit, their agile cleverness, their sensitive perception, their humorous appreciation, the saucy things they would say, and their pretty defiances', recalled one of his friends. But he fell in love deeply only once, with the beautiful Olivia, as he confessed to his clergyman's wife:

> I *am in love beyond all telling with the dearest and best girl in the world. I don't suppose she will marry me. I can't think it possible. She ought not to. But if she doesn't I shall still be sure that the best thing I ever did was to fall in love with her, and be proud to have it known that I tried to win her.*

There were tremendous obstacles in the way. Although now so admired as a leading American writer and humorist, Clemens had had a rough life working and tramping in the Mississippi region, and traces of it survived in his manner ever after. He was casual and irreverent; he didn't give a fig for parlour protocol, and would make himself a terror to maiden ladies by putting his feet up on their tables and draping his loose-jointed legs over their chairs. He was also an incorrigible prankster, and nothing was safe from his sense of the ridiculous. More seriously, he had no position and poor prospects. Stern Mr Langdon was not about to entrust his daisy-flower to such an unpromising reprobate.

But Clemens was a smart man. As soon as his feelings for Olivia were noticed on a visit, he was asked to leave. But *someone* had removed the bolts from the back seat of the family station wagon – so when the horse moved off, the passenger was tumbled out of the back. His resulting 'concussion' meant that he had to be carried back into the house, and nursed back to health – by Olivia!

Olivia herself was soon won. But her father was unconvinced. Finally he proposed that Clemens should provide some character references to establish his suitability as a husband. Clemens wrote at once to half a dozen worthy citizens who had been on good terms with him earlier in his life.

Naturally any friend of Clemens' would share his roistering sense of humour. All his referees obliged with outrageous replies stressing his rambunctious history and claiming that he would make about the worst husband since Bluebeard. Clemens was summoned to the Langdon house to hear the verdict passed on him by his 'supporters'. In his own words:

'I couldn't think of anything to say. Mr Langdon was apparently in the same condition. Finally he raised his handsome head, fixed his clear and candid eye upon me,

and said: "What kind of people are these? Haven't you a
friend in the world?"
    I said, "Apparently not."
    Then he said, "I'll be your friend myself. Take the girl.
I know you better than they do." '

And so the day was won. Mr Langdon never had cause to
regret his act of faith in the disreputable Clemens, who as
Mark Twain went on to carve out a great literary career for
himself with the same humour and dash that he had used
to win the woman he loved, and whom he never ceased to
love.

Popping The Question

Strange fits of passion I have known,
And I will dare to tell
But in the lover's ear alone
What once to me befell.

William Wordsworth

EVERY MAN HAS A PROPOSAL IN HIM — somewhere. But the process by which he winkles it out and drops it into the ear of his chosen one is shrouded in mystery. Proposing is one of the world's greatest secrets, like sex. Everyone knows that everyone else does it, but they never know exactly how and when. This is why, since you can't be doing it yourself all the time, there's a constant fascination with reading and talking about it.

The age-old interest in How To Do It comes out very clearly in all the old folk songs and ballads. For centuries these were the communal repository of wisdom and experience, before people were provided with soap opera as a guide to all human affairs. So there are countless songs in which 'a froggie would a-wooing go'. Sagas of frog courtship are not only confined to the pottier and more isolated areas of this sceptered isle. Cecil J. Sharp collected literally hundreds of these reptilian romances from all over the USA, froggies and toads a-wooing away like crazy.

A particularly fertile region was the Southern Appalachians, where one redoubtable matron gave Sharp no less than thiry-nine separate tunes. This lady was one Olive Dame Campbell by name, thus giving rise to the speculation that 'Dame' was not a handle but a title, awarded for her services to frog music. Admittedly, some of Dame Campbell's numbers are a bit samey. The basic tale of the amorous amphibian popping the question is cunningly recycled with different hilarious refrains, as here:

> *Gentleman Frog, he lived in the well,*
> *Hi ay de ling kum a laddy,*
> *A lady Mouse, she lived in the mill,*
> *Riddle I day, didn't I daddy.*

That one was recorded in Madison County, Kentucky, around the turn of this century. Another Kentucky frog song, from Claiborne County of the same period, has the even more compulsive refrain, 'Chow Willie, chow wee, chow willie wee, Rig tum a riddle lum a ree, chow willie wee' (makes you understand why they invented television, no?) But all these songs, by riddle, by ree, with a fol and a rol or whatever kind of lol, in the end get down to the nitty-gritty:

> *He took Missie Mouse upon his knee*
> *And he say, 'Missie Mouse, will you marry me?'*

Which of course, with the invaluable assistance of ol' Uncle Rat, she does.

Pursuing a suit matrimonial is not the sole prerogative of the cold-blooded species. Folk rhymesters have delighted in trying out this most basic of situations via other creatures as well. In a worn-out book of my childhood is a song that boasts itself as being old when Shakespeare was a little lad, and Mother Goose a slip of a gosling in short frocks:

THE HAPPY COURTSHIP, MERRY MARRIAGE, AND PICNIC DINNER OF COCK ROBIN AND JENNY WREN

Robin Redbreast lost his heart,
He was a gallant bird,
He doffed his hat to Jenny,
And thus to her he said:

My dearest Jenny Wren,
If you will but be mine,
You shall dine on cherry pie
And drink nice currant wine.

I'll dress you like a goldfinch,
Or like a peacock gay:
If you will have me, Jenny,
Let us appoint the day.

Jenny blushed behind her fan,
And thus declared her mind:
Then let it be tomorrow, Bob,
I take your offer kind.

Cherry pie is very good,
And so is currant wine.
But I will wear my russet gown
And never dress too fine.

So, with the help of all the birds of the air they are married, and Parson Rook pronounces the blessing:

Happy be the bridegroom,
Happy be the bride,
And may not man, nor bird, nor beast
This happy pair divide.

♡ 25 ♡

However many try-outs exist in folk versions, sooner or later folks have got to try it out for themselves – and it's not that easy. Everyone has to find their own initiation into the mystery, once again just like sex – but with this difference: that there aren't any proposing manuals or pillow-books to help the bashful and inexperienced male to glide through the mechanics of the act, and raise it to the level of an art. Like marriage itself, as described by the hero of *The Provoked Wife*, proposing is 'one great leap in the dark'. And all too many men simply close their eyes and jump!

One man who most uncharacteristically takes it at a jump is Mr Knightley, in Jane Austen's *Emma*. Knightley is nothing but grave and circumspect when it comes to other people's affairs, but when it comes to his own moment, it sort of steals up behind him and pushes him over the edge.

This proposal comes as a great surprise to both participants, since the lucky recipient herself does not see it coming. Emma is convinced that Mr Knightley is going to tell her off, as he has been a stern recording angel of her minor follies and vanities. So when she senses that Mr Knightley is on the brink of something, *'her immediate feeling was to avert the subject if possible.'*

But like murder, love will out:

Emma could not bear to give him pain . . . cost her what it would, she would listen . . .

'I stopped you ungraciously just now, Mr Knightley. If you have any wish to speak openly to me as a friend, or to ask my opinion of anything you have in contemplation – as a friend indeed you may command me. I will hear whatever you like. I will tell you exactly what I think.'

'As a friend!' repeated Mr Knightley. 'Emma, that I

♡ 26 ♡

fear is a word — No, I have no wish. Stay, yes, why should I hesitate? I have gone too far already for concealment. Emma, I accept your offer, extraordinary as it may seem, and refer myself to you as a friend. Tell me, then, have I no chance of ever succeeding?'

He stopped in his earnestness to look the question, and the expression of his eyes overpowered her.

'My dearest Emma,' said he, 'for dearest you will always be, whatever the event of this hour's conversation, my dearest, most beloved Emma — tell me at once. Say "no" if it is to be said.' She could really say nothing. 'You are silent!' he cried, with great animation; 'absolutely silent! At present I ask no more.'

Emma was ready to sink under the agitation of the moment . . .

With all these misunderstandings and difficulties, you can see why people will often try to back away from the big moment. Some will even rely on others to do it for them. Pop singer Cilla Black has had only one manager, Bobby Willis, for years. Suddenly they married, spurred on by a third party. As Cilla tells it with her bouncy Liverpudlian humour:

We were in a restaurant after a TV show, and we were having a row about something or other. A friend said we sounded just like man and wife, and asked why we didn't get wed. So we did!

And they have lived happily ever after.

Even when a girl is a little more prepared than Emma, she will not necessarily be any more at home with this great mystery. The idea may have been around, but the moment will still take her by surprise. Many writers have seen the warm comic potential of a man and woman in love who join hands and make the leap marriage-wards together, almost without knowing how they've done it. A dearly-loved American classic in this vein is *The Courtin'*, a specimen of 'Down East Humour' that was popular in the nineteenth century — though about as far removed from Jane Austen's world as it is possible to be:

> *Zekle crep' up quite unbeknown*
> *An' peeked in through the winder.*
> *An' there sot Huldy, quite alone,*
> *With no-one nigh to hinder.*
>
> *She heered a foot, an' knowed it too,*
> *A-raspin' on the scraper —*
> *All ways to once her feelins flew*
> *Like sparks to burnt up paper.*

Huldy has a pretty good idea what Zekle has come for. Her heart goes out to him as he 'kinda loiters' on the mat, won't come in, and she can hear *his* heart thumping right across the room. But she doesn't want to seem too easy, and so resorts to a provoking indifference:

> *'You want to see my Pa, I spose?'*
>   *'Wal . . . no . . . I come designin' '* —
> *'To see my Ma? She's sprinklin' cloes*
> *Agin tomorrer's i'nin' '*
>
> *Says he, 'I'd better call agin;'*
> *Says she, 'Think likely, Mister.'*
> *That last word pricked him like a pin,*
> *An' . . . wal, he up an' kist her!*
>
> *Then her red come up like the tide,*
> *Down to the Bay o' Fundy.*
> *An' all I know is, they wuz cried*
> *In meetin' come nex' Sunday!*

♡ 28 ♡

So a marriage has been arranged. Zekle has asked Huldy, and she has accepted him. But the mystery persists. How did he do it? What did she say? To these perennial questions let the inimitable Jane Austen have the last word, on Emma's reaction to Mr Knightley's proposal:

What did she say? Just what she ought, of course. A lady always does.

Of course!

The Way It Used To Be

'Suffer me, suffer me then,' cried he with warmth, 'to hasten the time when none shall longer harbour any doubt — when your grateful Orville may call you all his own!'

Fanny Burney, *Evelina*

IT'S ALL VERY WELL being crept up on, when the marriage moment takes both partners by surprise. But there's no doubt that both women and men love a little more formality on this extra-special occasion. Romantics look back wistfully to the Good Old Days, when a proposal of marriage was a serious business, and taken seriously by all concerned.

For once upon a time, love came before the joys of sex so speedily delivered today. In those days the Ultimate Experience that maidens sighed for and blushed about was the offer of marriage. Masculine anxiety about 'how to do it' referred not to the intricacies of the primal act, but the necessity of making a proposal and making it a good one.

Any modern man could take lessons from Lord Orville, above. His is an absolute cracker of a proposal, old-style — a full-dress version as against the full-frontal that girls are favoured with today. He has courted Evelina throughout the book, remaining constant through all the troubles that, as a heroine, she inevitably has to undergo. Finally he approaches to claim the hand of his 'too lovely friend', as Evelina herself tells it:

> '*My Lord!*' *cried I, endeavouring to disengage my hand,* '*pray let me go!*'
>
> '*I will,*' *cried he, to my inexpressible confusion dropping on one knee,* '*if you wish to leave me.*'
>
> '*Oh, my Lord,*' *exclaimed I,* '*rise, I beseech you, rise! — surely your Lordship is not so cruel as to mock me!*'
>
> '*Mock you!*' *repeated he earnestly;* '*no, I revere you! I esteem and admire you above all human beings! you are the friend to whom my soul is attached as its better half! you are the most amiable of women! and you are dearer to me than language has power of telling!*'
>
> *I attempt not to describe my sensations at that moment; I scarcely breathed; I doubted if I existed — the blood forsook my cheeks, and my feet refused to sustain me. Lord Orville, hastily rising, supported me to a chair, upon which I sunk almost lifeless.*
>
> *For a few moments we neither of us spoke . . . the moment my strength returned I was not proof against his solicitations — and he drew from me the most sacred secret of my heart!*

Now isn't that marvellous? Classic, in fact, his lordship dropping elegantly to *one* knee instead of thundering down on two, to the accompaniment of a cracking of cartilage whose report would drop a rhino at twenty paces. And the noble lord has got hold of the idea that the classic proposal should be garnished with lavish helpings of praise and compliment. You may not exactly demand that the chap should be muttering 'it is a marvel that those red rose-leaf lips of yours should be made no less for the music of song than the madness of kissing', or 'your slim-gilt soul walks between passion and poetry', but the odd bucketful of adulation is definitely *de rigueur*.

Lord Orville's stylish wooing is all the more remarkable considering that the British upper crust are generally held to be rather poor at all the lovey-dovey stuff (stiff upper lips not being quite formed for the madness of kissing and all that). Their finest flights are supposed to be such as: *What say, old gel? Make a go of it, shall we? Tie the knot, eh?* with which one hunting peer of the Midlands says he won his countess many moons ago.

But Oscar Wilde believed that the British upper classes *were* good at it. His own luscious wooing of Lord Alfred Douglas, quoted above, suggests that he knew something of the case. At the very least, he did them the compliment of demonstrating how good they might be, if only they'd let themselves!

Few writers have handled the marriage proposal with more affection and panache than Wilde. His plays abound in the attempts of keen young men to secure the ever-wavering attentions of their bright young women. In his masterpiece, *The Importance of Being Earnest*, proposing is established as the chief concern of the play and everyone in it, from the very first scene:

ALGERNON: *How are you, my dear Ernest? What brings you to town?*

JACK: *Oh, pleasure, pleasure! What else should bring one anywhere? I am in love with Gwendolen. I have come to town expressly to propose to her.*

ALGERNON: *I thought you had come up for pleasure? I call that business.*

JACK: *How utterly unromantic you are!*

Before very long the tables are turned on the heretic Algy.

♡ 32 ♡

He falls madly in love, and has to eat his own sceptical words. He also learns the truth of film-maker François Truffaut's statement:

> *In love, men are amateurs, women the professionals.*

For Algy's beloved, Cecily, is streets ahead of him in the wooing dance:

ALGERNON: *I hope, Cecily, I shall not offend you if I state quite frankly that you seem to me the visible personification of absolute perfection.*

CECILY: *Your frankness does you great credit.*

ALGERNON: *Cecily, ever since I first looked upon your wonderful and incomparable beauty, I have dared to love you wildly, passionately, devotedly, hopelessly . . . You will marry me, won't you?*

CECILY: *You silly boy! Of course. Why, we have been engaged for the last three months.*

ALGERNON: *(bewildered) But how did we become engaged?*

CECILY: *Well, ever since Uncle Jack first confessed to me that he had a younger brother who was very wicked and bad, I dare say it was foolish of me, but I fell in love with you.*

ALGERNON: *Darling. And when was the engagement actually settled?*

CECILY: *On the 14th of February last. Worn out by your entire ignorance of my existence, I determined to end the matter one way or another, and after a long struggle with myself I accepted you under this dear old tree here. The next day I bought this little ring in your name, and this is the bangle with the true lovers' knot I promised you always to wear . . . And this is the box in which I keep all your dear letters tied up with blue ribbon.*

♡ 33 ♡

ALGERNON: *My letters! But my own sweet Cecily, I have never written you any letters.*

CECILY: *You need hardly remind me of that! I remember only too well that I was forced to write your letters for you, always three times a week and sometimes oftener.*

ALGERNON: *What a perfect angel you are, Cecily?*

Signed, sealed, delivered. Cecily's dazzling adroitness at tying the knot, in the absence and without the knowledge of her intended, can only evoke the purest admiration. Sheer professionalism, that's what it is. Wilde more than once makes the observation that men often propose for practice. Judging from Cecily's expertise, they must all propose to the same girls!

That is certainly the experience of the heroine of Judith Krantz' *Scruples*, the fabulously sexy Billy Winthrop, who learns from her best friend Jessica to rate her men out of ten, and keeps score in quite the literalest sense of the word:

Billy had seven proposals of marriage from nines she didn't love, and, reluctantly, she had to replace them. It would not have been playing the game fairly to keep them on the string after honourable intentions had been declared. Jessica had twelve proposals in the same period of time, but they decided that it amounted to an even number, because only men over six feet tall proposed to Billy, while tiny Jessica had a much wider field to appeal to.

In a straightforward reversal of old-time practice, the declaration of honourable intent is, for all these men, the way out of their ladies' beds, rather than the way *in*! They just have to go when they get serious. But for the girls, as Liddy says in Hardy's *Far From the Madding Crowd*, 'How sweet to be able to disdain!' And maybe even 'nines', sexually speaking, have not cracked the art of proposing to as opposed to pleasuring a woman.

And maybe, too, more attention is given to the old-style proposal in the Old World than in the New. Henry James constantly says:

> *the English are the most romantic people in the world.*

He shares Wilde's faith in the powers of the upper social echelons if not to get the girl, at least to get the offer right. Here is the altogether too divine Lord Warburton in *Portrait Of A Lady*. He is not only a poppet in himself, but further adorned with a hundred thousand a year (pounds, not dollars), fifty thousand acres, half a dozen stately homes, and cultivated tastes in literature, art and science to boot. And in addition, his lordship can propose as to the manor born:

> *. . . said Lord Warburton, 'I care only for you.'*
>
> *'You have known me too short a time to have a right to say that, and I cannot believe you are serious.'*
>
> *'One's right in such a matter is not measured by the time, Miss Archer, it is measured by the feeling itself . . . Of course I have seen you very little, but my impression dates from the very first hour we met. I lost no time; I fell in love with you then . . . nothing you said, nothing you did, was lost on me. All these days I have thought of nothing else.*
>
> *'I don't go off easily, but when I am touched, it's for life. It's for life, Miss Archer, it's for life,' Lord Warburton repeated in the kindest, tenderest, pleasantest voice Isabel had ever heard, and looking at her with eyes that shone with the light of a passion that had sifted itself clear of the baser parts of emotion — the heat, the violence, the unreason — and which burned as steadily as a lamp in a windless*

place . . . 'If you will be my wife, then I shall know you,
and when I tell you all the good I think of you, you will
not be able to say it is from ignorance.'

Oh, the love! How can she resist? For she does, dear
reader, she does! Henry James probably overloads the
worldly attractions — even for a lord, Warburton seems to
have a few houses, acres and ackers over the odds — but he
does succeed in making him such a pie-faced sweetheart
that you could just eat him up. This is the first time in the
book, but not the last, that you want to give Isabel a good
shake — along with the instruction that if she disdains her
lovely lord, she should pass him on to someone who will
appreciate him!

So it's not quite true as the old proverb says that 'all the
world loves a lord'. But it's nice to know that lordly
proposals, old-style, do still come off even in this day and
age. In her cheerful autobiography, *Nicole Nobody*, the
unjustly self-styled 'nobody' describes her courtship by the
present Duke of Bedford, lord of Woburn Abbey. Nicole
Milinaire had lived life to the full, through good times and
bad. She had survived an unhappy marriage, the wartime
fall of her beloved France, and lived to make it as a TV
producer and business woman in France, England and
America. Along the way she met Ian, Duke of Bedford,
one new face among many in her busy life:

> *. . . I flew to Hollywood to discuss a picture deal, and*
> *returned to London on 2 October.*
>
> *I arrived back desperately tired. I wanted to shut out the*
> *world, take a bath and go to sleep. The doorbell rang. I*
> *opened the door gingerly. It was the Duke of Bedford. I*
> *was amazed to see him, because at that point we were*
> *acquaintances rather than friends . . .*

*I noticed for the first time that he had an enormous
bouquet of white lilies half hidden behind his back.*

'What's so special about today?' I asked.

*Ian looked down at me with a singularly tender look.
He has an almost superhuman gentleness when he wishes,
and in his slow, hesitant way he said:*

'I have come to ask you to marry me.'

*In crises, in moments of great joy, I laugh . . . I
laughed and laughed and parried:*

'Won't you settle for a drink instead?'

Naturally Nicole felt some hesitation. The responsibility
of becoming chatelaine of Woburn Abbey daunted her
and, touchingly, she also wanted to know what her
children thought of the idea. But then she accepted him:

*We laughed a lot together, and to this day I tell him that
that is why I married him . . . I knew that my life
without him would be empty. He had become so much a
part of it, with his gentle manners, his soft sense of
humour, his wit, that when we were apart I missed him
not a little, but very much. It was as simple as that. He
had become indispensable to my happiness.*

And that's what it's all about, isn't it?

The Way Of A Man With A Maid

Yonder a maid and her wight
Go whispering by,
War's annals will fade into night
Ere their story die.

Thomas Hardy

IT'S LOVELY WHEN DUKES FIND their Duchesses. Or any kind of lord or lordling, baron or baronet. But making a magic proposal is not the monopoly of a titled or educated man. The wonders of falling in love and wanting to marry are available to all comers, high and low alike. It's a real-life drama of dreams come true for every new couple.

The proposals of un-literary men have a vigour and directness that make you want to jump up and accept them, straight off. As Miss Matty says in *Cranford*:

I have known people with very good hearts and clever minds too, who were not what some people reckoned refined, but who were both true and tender.

True and tender is the very phrase for the unknown suitor who composed his proposal in verse some time in the seventeenth century. This wonderful little poem survives only in a hand-written commonplace book, and the lover

♡ 38 ♡

is identified only as 'Jan' — a common name for a man until
it died out around 1850.

Jan's lady is obviously a woman of spirit. Notice how
often he keeps promising her that she can wear the trousers
if she likes. He's also keen to assure her that she will be
treated with all the respect that a husband owes his wife.
But the amorous undertone on his reference to her 'fair
bum' suggests that he won't neglect his other matrimonial
responsibilities either:

> *I am by fate slave to your will,*
> *And I will be obedient still.*
> *To show my love I will compose ye*
> *For your fair finger's ring, a posie,*
> *In which shall be expressed my duty*
> *And how I'll be forever true t'ye;*
> *With low-made bows and sugared speeches,*
> *Yielding to your fair bum the breeches,*
> *And show myself in all I can*
>
> > **Your very humble servant**
> >
> > ### JAN

Jan might have been an ordinary man, but he'd got hold
of one very important truth — that a female does like to
have her . . . *understanding* admired. In the famous case
that rocked British racing, was it disqualifiable conduct
when a gentleman jockey rode up behind a lady jockey and
sang out '**WHAT-A-LOVELY-BOTTOM!**', thus causing
her to lose her concentration (and the race)?

Sometimes men who are not inclined to flowery verbiage
find that actions speak louder than words. Shelley Winters
records that her first husband was a flying enthusiast, who
used to take her up in small open-cockpit aeroplanes.
When she proved that she wasn't frightened, but loved

flying as much as he did, he knew what to do. He whizzed her off one Sunday somewhere over Cleveland, and presumably having switched over to the automatic pilot, he slipped a beautiful 3-carat diamond ring on her finger. 'I still wear it,' she says with satisfaction. Now that's the kind of gesture most girls would appreciate!

But of all the speaking actions in the history of marriage proposals, surely the most endearing is that of 'Major Jones'. Major Jones flourished in the old South West of America in the 1840s and was the creation of a refugee Northerner, William Tappan Thompson. As the hard-pressed editor of a failing periodical, Thompson invented this character of a lovable innocent in a last-ditch effort to save his paper. The paper folded anyway, but the Major lived on.

The story of 'Major Jones's Courtship' is told in a series of letters which have lost none of their appeal today. Part of their charm lies in the Major's unique style of writing. With a sublime unselfconsciousness, he makes up all his own spelling and grammar as he goes along. It's not that he's ignorant or stupid. Born into the Southern gentry, with his own plantation and the future set fair, he just has had no call to be overloaded with book-larnin'.

But with or without benefit of Webster's Dictionary, young Joseph Jones is a simply gorgeous catch. He is straight, sweet, and honest as the day is long. He knows how to love a girl, and how to show her what he can't put into words. This is how he does it. One Christmas Eve he pays a call on the beautiful Miss Mary, to tell her about the Christmas present that he wants to give her:

> *'I got a gift for you, what I want you to keep all your life, but it would take a two-bushel bag to hold it,' ses I.*
> *'Oh, that's the kind,' ses she.*

'But will you keep it as long as you live?' ses I.

'Certinly I will, Majer,' ses Miss Mary, 'but what is it?'

'Never mind,' ses I. 'You hang up a bag big enuff to hold it, and you'll find out what it is, when you see it in the mornin.'

I sot up till mid night, and when they was all gone to bed I went softly into the back gate, and went up to the porch, and thar, shore enuff, was a grate big meal bag hangin to the jice. It was monstrous unhandy to git into it, but I was tarmined not to back out. I sot down in bag, and here cum Missis' grate big cur dog rippin and tarin through the yard like rath. I didn't breathe louder nor a kitten, for fear he'd find me out.

This South-West version of the Hound of the Baskervilles barks and sniffs round him all night. The Major hangs there in mortal dread that any second he will feel a vicious set of canines sink into the seat of his pants. But this is not the only trial. If ever a man suffered . . .

The wind begun to blow bominable cold, and the old bag kep turnin round and swingin so it made me sea-sick as mischief . . . thar I sot with my teeth rattlin like I had a ager. I do blieve if I didn't love Miss Mary so powerful I would of froze to deth; for my hart was the only spot that felt warm, and it didn't beat more'n two licks a minit, only when I thought how she would be sprised in the mornin, and then it went into a canter.

At last morning comes, and the sack is found and opened:

'Good Gracious!' ses Miss Mary, 'if it ain't the Majer himself!'

'Yes!' ses I. 'And you know you promised to keep my Crismus present as long as you lived.'

♡ 41 ♡

Miss Mary — bless her bright eyes — she blushed as butiful as a morninglory and sed she'd stick to her word. I tell you what, it was worth hangin in a meal bag from one Crismus to another to feel as happy as I done ever since.

You must come to the weddin if you possibly kin. I'll let you know when. No more from,

Yore frend till deth,

JOS. JONES

What about Jos, then? Isn't he a peach? If this is what men were like in the ol' Deep South, no wonder Scarlett O'Hara wanted to get back to the plantation. So next Christmas, when you're hanging up your stocking, don't forget to suspend a two-bushel meal bag somewhere prominent outside — just in case there are any more Jones boys at home like the darling 'Majer'!

A man in love will often express himself all the better for being natural and unaffected. Such a man is Kester Woodseaves, the hero of Mary Webb's unforgettable novel, *Precious Bane*. This recounts the story of Prudence Sarn, a country girl with a fiercely loving heart and a deep longing to have a mate of her own, a cottage and 'a babe in a cot o' rushes'. But her looks are marred by one blemish, like a scar on her sensitive soul — she has a hare lip. Because of this, she is brutally told, she will never have a husband or lover, 'her own dear acquaintance' in the country dialect that she speaks. Prue tells us how this makes her feel in her own simple yet poetic way:

I was like a maid standing at the meeting of the lane-ends on May Day with a posy-knot as a favour for a rider that should come by. And behold! The horseman rode straight over me, and left me, posy and all, in the mire.

Then Kester Woodseaves comes into her life, and she

knows at once that her soul has found its mate – 'here was my lover and my lord'. But she has no hope of winning him, handsome, merry and kind as he is, and goes out of her way to keep her love secret. Yet Kester is drawn to this shy, passionate girl, and tries to show her his awakening love:

> . . . *It seemed to me, though I told myself it must be fancy, that his eyes, so live and bright, dwelt on me, smiled at me, friended me and pled with me, being as are the eyes of a man when he looks long upon his dear acquaintance who has given her peace for his, her soul to his keeping, and her body for his joy.*

Kester is determined to break down Prue's resistance to him, and convince her that she is attractive. He refuses to let her call herself 'a poor daggly creature', and tells her that she has 'a figure like an apple-blossom fairy'. Tenderly but firmly he moves her towards the realization that they were meant for one another:

> *'You still go frommet me a bit, I see, Prue Sarn. It mun be toerts, not frommet.'*

Prue still finds it almost impossible to believe that she can be moving 'towards' such undreamed-of happiness, not away 'frommet'. But finally, in the powerful climax of the story, Kester comes riding by to claim her as his 'dear acquaintance', his lover and his wife:

> *'Prue!' he said.*
> *I rose up.*
> *'Did I say at harvesting that it was to be toerts or frommet?' he asked me.*
> *'Toerts.'*
> *I could only whisper it.*

♡ 43 ♡

'*Come here, then, Prue Woodseaves!*'

He stooped. He set his arms about me. He lifted me to the saddle. All sank, all faded in the quiet air. There was only the evening wind lifting the boughs, like a lover lifting his maid's long hair. We were going at a canter towards the blue and purple mountains.

'*But no!*' *I said.* '*It mun be frommet, Kester. You mun marry a girl like a lily. See, I be hare-shotten!*'

But he wouldna listen. He wouldna argufy. Only after I'd pleaded agen myself a long while, he pulled up sharp, and looking down into my eyes, he said —

'*No more sad talk! I've chosen my bit of Paradise. 'Tis on your breast, my dear acquaintance!*'

And when he'd said those words, he bent his comely head and kissed me full on the mouth.

What man could better that?

7

Short and Simple

'Barkis is willin''
Charles Dickens, *David Copperfield*

A PROPOSAL IS USUALLY SOMETHING of a ceremony. A man knows that he has a part to play and must play it in style. Most will look for the occasion or the setting that will enhance their chances, and lend sparkle to the start of the new relationship. They may feel the need to offer, promise, blandish or cajole. They try to sell themselves with a bit of a flourish, or at least to appear an attractive prospect at this great moment.

But others take quite the opposite attitude. They want to cut the cackle and get down to business with the absolute minimum of flummery. No long speeches, moonlight scenes or earth-shaking exchanges for them — the briefer the better is their motto. Just look in any national newspaper on St Valentine's Day for the annual crop of simple proposals. 'MARRY ME' demand the current suitors. It's impossible to tell from this if they ask in hope or despair, but they certainly ask in the shortest way possible.

If brevity is the soul of wit, there surely are some witty proposals on record. A hot contender for the brevity *and* wit award must be the cryptic line that appeared in a British travel magazine in 1981:

Writer seeks 'wife' for year on desert island.

This offer emanated from writer Gerald Kingsland, who had found his plans to go and live on a desert island thwarted for the want of a wife. This situation is not unfamiliar to butlers, MPs, rising young executives and suchlike – nothing like a little woman (the right little woman) to add lustre to a chap whose Tinkerbell quotient is a shade dim by itself.

Such was not Mr Kingsland's case, who had no thought of impressing selection committees and their ilk on his desert island. 'The wife, he hoped, could supply some help and comfort on the adventure,' according to the *Sunday Telegraph*. He considerately put the word 'wife' in inverted commas in his advert, to indicate that applicants did not have to marry him if they didn't want to.

Naturally he was not short of candidates for this interesting post. The successful wife-to-be was Lucy Irvine, 25, and both lovely and talented enough to dispel any suspicion that she was only doing it to get out of the Inland Revenue, where she happened to be employed at the time. And yes, reader, she married him. Their Cupid, marriage-broker or go-between turned out to be the Australian Immigration Department, who would not issue visas, even for a desert island, to those who intended to live there in sin. So Mrs Kingsland Lucy became, and writer Gerald scored 100% success with his nifty proposal.

Other people, of course, don't have such exotic lives, or such good reasons as 30p per word for keeping their offers to the minimum. But the reasons for not coming over all unnecessary can be just as valid. One old Warwickshire farmer says that he won his wife in 'a straight plain downright way o' dealin' ':

> *Well, us 'ud courted near on four year. We wus fourteen when I seen 'er first, bringin' 'er dad's cows 'ome over Meriden way. I seen 'er like one o' them roses, straw 'at and all pink. I never wanted no other. So I courted her, like, and abided me time, and 'twarn't easy. 'Er dad were an old devil. But I knew me time when it come, and I just looked 'er in the eye and I says, 'Sall us, old girl?'*
>
> *'Er wus eighteen then. And 'er says "Ar". And that wus it!*

At the other end of the scale is the true-life story of a junior ornament of the British social scene, then in his final year as an undergraduate at Oxford. He was quite legendary for his stinginess with words. His entire repartee consisted of 'What?', 'Har', and 'Get orf!' When ribbed about this (which he was, brutally and often) he fell back on his ancient family motto. This was an encrusted hunk of Latin which roughly translated as 'Let the other fellows shoot their mouths off, then whip in and make the killing'. Only briefer, of course.

Our hero laid this motto to his heart, and proceeded to act upon it when the moment came to make an offer of his triple-barrelled name and rather personable person to the lady of his choice. They were well matched, as she had the effervescent wit and sparkling personality of the average clam. But the taciturn speak each other's language. So she knew what he meant when he took her out to Oxford's poshest restaurant, ordered champagne, and just as it was being opened said to her in all simplicity:

Pop!

It might reflect more credit on his modesty had he popped

the question *as* a question, rather than as a statement. But he didn't. And like all good couples, *they* knew what they were doing. It never even occurred to her to enter him for the *Guinness Book of Records* with the Shortest Proposal Ever. She just accepted him with one languid lift of an eyebrow, and they've lived quietly ever since.

The favourite of the economy offerings, though, must be the superb Dickensian moment, 'Barkis is willin' '. It's interesting to notice that the line as it stands is quite neutral. You can even imagine it said by some horrible villain to one of Dickens' innocent rosebud heroines: 'Barkis is willin', m' dear, ha ha!' he goes with a dastardly twirl of his tash, as she shudders, clasps her little hands, and rolls her forget-me-not eyes heavenwards.

But Barkis is a horse of another colour. He's not a man to force himself on any woman. It takes him all his time to hint at his intentions via young David: *'If you was writin' to her, p'raps you'd recollect to say that Barkis was willin': would you?'*

Thus young David becomes the messenger boy, innocently writing these funny little missives to his nurse, Peggotty, which consist largely of 'Barkis is willing, P.S. BARKIS IS WILLING!'

As in all true love stories, the course of Barkis's wooing is neither smooth nor swift. He has to keep prompting his little Mercury to repeat the message. Later he has to prod the fair Peggotty, now promoted to 'Clara' in his affections, with the fresh instruction that:

> *When a man says he's willin', it's as much as to say, that man's a-waitin' for an answer.*

Peggotty is not easily won. She vigorously drats his impudence, and protests that she wouldn't have him if he was made of gold, not she! From which we gather that she has determined to accept him, and so she does. And they, too, live happily ever after.

As this suggests, a ready wit and constant flow of speech are by no means essential to the task of proposing. Men who don't normally say boo to a goose can make a perfect success of their proposals, and of their subsequent marriages, too. And good luck to them all!

What A Nerve!

'I want to ask you a question.'
'What?' I said, in a small unpromising voice.
'How would you like to be Mrs Buddy Willard?'

Sylvia Plath, *The Bell Jar*

'MAN PROPOSES, GOD DISPOSES', runs the proverb. 'And women have to put up with the mess they both make of it', as one of England's premier duchesses observes in her irreverent moments. Since society and custom have traditionally favoured *men* with the right of proposing, all too often women are no more than sitting ducks — and there are some terrible bird dogs around.

It is a myth that women are the ones who are wild to get married, while the noble male has his mind loftily fixed on higher things. Men unthinkingly expect to marry, to replace painlessly the services of their mother with the more extended range of functions that a wife can provide. Therefore they get really nervous when they realize that it's not just going to *happen* — or rather, that it seems to be happening to all their chums and not to them. Hooray Henries are converted overnight into Desperate Dans, who now get you up a corner at a party to confide gloomily that they've missed the boat, all the good ones have gone, and do you think they ought to have a go at old Sarah before that wally Henderson snaffles her up?

In such moods men will propose to anything. One young Warwickshire squire spent all his time with his horses and hounds, and his conversational level was about on a par with that of his four-footed friends. Not surprisingly, his efforts to get a girl to share his life went unrewarded. After recognizing his failure he was in danger of moving from the equestrian class to the neurotic, in G.B. Shaw's memorable division of English society. He was overheard at the County Horse Show, frenziedly outlining to his thoroughbred mare all the reasons why he'd make a terrific husband, and concluding with:

Dammit all, Tosca, YOU'D have me, wouldn't you?

Yet whether impelled by desperation or deep self-love, men still go on proposing. You may heartily agree that they need all the practice they can get but, as with sex, you're likely to have serious reservations about being the party practised upon. What woman can enjoy being at the mercy of a guy whose fumbling inexpertise raises incompetence to the level of an art? Yet this is what happens, all the time.

Fearless and painstaking research has uncovered a vast number of Truly Awful Proposals. Some of these specimens are so choice as to qualify as anti-proposals. How would you feel on the receiving end of any of these?

♡ *'I'll marry you, I know I'm stuck with you for life'*
♡ *'I've decided we should marry — for tax purposes'*
♡ *'We have to get married — I'm sick of buying you things and having to be nice to you all the time!'*

As this shows, your researcher never failed to boldly go where no man has gone before, in asking women about men asking them to marry. It can now be reported that in all the above cases, every single one of these dreadful drongos was *accepted*!

It's not easy to be a star of the marriage moment. Being a real star, even a movie hero of zillions of women's romantic fantasies, doesn't mean you can do in your own life what you do so superbly on celluloid. The amazing Peter Finch had as his first love a beautiful Australian socialite called Sheila (really). He took her out dancing to create the right atmosphere – 'Peter simply was *the* most gorgeous dancer,' she says – but when it came to the point, all he could do was blurt out:

We must get married!

Yet even this effort makes Finchie look like a king of chivalry against Richard Burton. The Welsh wizard, far from proposing to the most famous of his wives, assaulted Elizabeth Taylor with a barrage of insults from the word go, of which 'Miss Tits', 'fat little tart' and 'she's so dark she probably shaves' are among the more fragrant samples.

The real enemy of promise among proposing males is a massive masculine arrogance. This means a complete blindness to the rights and needs of the woman, even when they are protesting that they love her above all the world.

Henry James made a study of such a man in *The Bostonians*. Basil Ransom's 'love' for Verena Tarrant means a determination to get her away from her parents, from the life she leads with her lesbian friend Olive, and especially from her work in the emerging movement for women's rights in America. She resists his attentions, even goes into hiding to get away from him, but he catches up with her just as she is about to address a public meeting. He knows at once that he is on the point of victory:

He saw that he could do what he wanted, that she begged him, with all her being to spare her, but that so long as he should protest, she was submissive, helpless . . .

'Dearest, I told you, I warned you. I left you alone for ten weeks; but could that make you doubt it was coming? Not for words, not for millions, shall you give yourself to that roaring crowd. Don't ask me to care for them or for anyone! You are mine, not theirs!'

Brutally Ransome fights off all remonstration, all reproach: 'do you suppose I pretend not to be selfish?' he demands. 'She's mine or she isn't, and if she's mine she's all mine.' Even the pleas of Verena herself have no impact on him:

'Oh, let me off, let me off . . . it's too terrible, it's impossible. Now I want you to go away — I will see you tomorrow, as long as you wish. That's all I want now; if you will only go away it's not too late, and everything will be alright!'

In answer, Ransome simply states:

We shall catch the night train for New York, and the first thing in the morning we shall be married.

He wrenches her away 'by muscular force', and is proud and happy at his success. But Verena, beneath her cloak, is in tears. And as James gravely observes in a heart-stopping final sentence:

It is to be feared that with the union, so far from brilliant, into which she was about to enter, these were not the last she was destined to shed.

When a man has resolved to marry a woman above all else, he will usually succeed in overriding her objections. The woman, caught between bafflement and fear, is mesmerized by the dark satanic drive of the man, and cannot hold out against him. This is the setting for Shakespeare's most famous marriage proposal, in *Richard III*.

Richard, especially as played by Laurence Olivier in the film version, is the favourite villain of English history, the one we all love to hate. In Shakespeare's play he takes time out from marmolizing the Little Princes in the Tower to develop all his other gifts in the murder and mayhem department. Chatting to the audience about his famous hunch back, Richard declares that he's not cut out to be the Errol Flynn of the Wars of the Roses:

> *And therefore, since I cannot prove a lover,*
> *I am determined to prove a villain!*

But in a tense and completely unexpected development, he contrives to be both, simultaneously! Fresh from plotting death and destruction all round, Richard weaves a new plan:

> *For now I'll marry Warwick's youngest daughter.*
> *What though I killed her husband, and her father?*
> *The readiest way to make the wench amends*
> *Is to become her husband and her father.*

As luck would have it, Richard runs down his proposed bride, the Lady Anne, in the presence of yet another of his victims, King Henry VI. And in a terrifically effective *coup de théâtre* he makes love to her over the still-bleeding corpse and claims her as his own.

The Lady Anne is by no means a pushover. As soon as Richard appears she flies at him with threats and curses, calling him a 'devil', a 'villain', and a 'lump of foul deformity'. Yet the more she rages, the more steadily Richard advances his suit. He tells her that the best place in the world for him is her bed, and finally orders her,

'Vouchsafe to wear this ring'. Exhausted and out-man-oeuvred, she takes it and with it Richard himself. As he gloats afterwards:

> *Was ever woman in this humour wooed?*
> *Was ever woman in this humour won?*

Fortunately, some women in this situation hang onto their native bottle, even if they don't quite manage to smash it over the proposer's head. A prototype of the plucky little woman is the heroine of *Jane Eyre*. Like her creator, Charlotte Brontë, Jane is more likely to give a man a sock on the kisser than a kiss on the feet. She is being pressurized to marry by her cousin, St John Rivers. He does not love her, but sees her as a mainstay of his plan to go out to India and convert 'the heathen':

> As *a conductress of Indian schools, and a helper among Indian women, your assistance will be invaluable.*

Sounds grim, doesn't it? No wonder we lost the Empire, as my father used to say when confronted with any manifestation of modern life from decimal coinage to the Rolling Stones. You need only feel sorry for the Indian objects of St John's forthcoming mission. For Jane needs no sympathy. She listens carefully to his proposal:

> *God and nature intended you for a missionary's wife. It is not personal, but mental endowments they have given you: you are formed for labour, not for love. A missionary's wife you must — you shall be. You shall be mine: I claim you — not for my pleasure, but for my Sovereign's service.*

Then she gives him his just deserts for such a romantic and loving proposal – in plain English, the boot!

> *'I scorn your idea of love,' I could not help saying as I*

*rose up and stood before him, 'I scorn the counterfeit senti-
ment you offer: yes, St John, and I scorn you when you offer
it!'*

That's the stuff. Right, left, and the uppercut straight to
the jaw. Attagirl!

All these shuddersome proposals have one thing in
common. They aren't, truly, proposals in the real sense,
since the men never actually *ask*. They decide, declare,
and assume possession, following the Julius Caesar model
of manly conduct — came, saw and overcame. This is
probably the most insulting way a man can 'propose' to a
woman — apart from telling her in the process that she is
as plain as a pikestaff and made for use, not ornament, as
St John does to Jane above.

This type of back-hander is just what the heroine Sybilla
gets in the award-winning Australian movie, *My Brilliant
Career*. The would-be masterful male here is in fact a
Snotty Pommy, which may or may not be an improvement
upon the Whingeing Pom from the Antipodean point of
view. Against an appropriate background of sheep, Sybilla
has to listen to his silly bleating:

POM: *I enjoyed myself last night. I thought we got on
jolly well together. Sybilla — I've been thinking. Well —
looks aren't everything —*

SYBILLA: *Would you come to the point, Frank?*

POM: *Well, now that this fellow Harry has gone, you
should pay some heed to my attentions.*

SYBILLA: *Do you mean attentions or intentions?*

POM: *At the conclusion of the coming year, I shall be
returning to England, and I expect you to return with
me as my wife.*

At which point Sybilla shows her estimation of his proposal

by pushing him in the sheep pen in a tough but necessary rejoinder.

For if they don't ask, but just presume, it takes nerve and guts to get them to understand, let alone accept, a refusal. This is the dilemma of Elizabeth Bennet in *Pride and Prejudice*, the most enchanting of Jane Austen's heroines for her quicksilver gaiety and her loving heart. Neither of these qualities is to be detected in her would-be husband Mr Collins, like St John Rivers a creepy clergyman of nauseous piety and hypocritical cant.

This prize nerd is due to inherit the Bennet estate as the nearest male heir. In a conceited plan to make up to Elizabeth and her sisters for this naked act of male chauvinist highway robbery, Mr Collins has decided to make one of them his wife. Pick a sister, any sister, is his system – he's not particular.

Nothing on earth could make him even tolerable in Elizabeth's eyes. She has been enjoying him as a joke, but now she finds to her horror that the joke's on her. She can't bear him. But how to give him the bum's rush?

Elizabeth tries various methods of refusing him, but Mr Collins has somehow absorbed from the pulp fiction of his day the idea that in True Romance the lady always refuses the man she secretly intends to accept at least six times. And then there's Mr Collins' ace in the hole, Lady Catherine de Bourgh. He has been so puffed up by the patronage of this small-time noblewoman, to whom he toadies shamelessly for advancement, that it never occurs to him that a lesser gentlewoman could find him unattractive.

All this emerges clearly from his proposal, a parade of such bare-faced ego-mania that Elizabeth might just as well not be present at all. Mr Collins makes love to himself, and at the end of his proposal is not at all surprised to find himself accepted, all over bar the shouting:

> *Almost as soon as I entered the house, I singled you out as the companion of my future life. But before I am run away with by my feelings on this subject, perhaps it will be advisable for me to state my reasons for coming into Hertfordshire with the design of selecting a wife.*

Felicitous touch that 'selecting', eh? Makes lovely Lizzie sound like a box of chocs or a piece of fruit. But Mr Collins is very hot on the *mot juste*, especially of the heavyweight Latin variety, as follows:

> *Now nothing remains for me but to assure you in the most animated language of the violence of my affection. To fortune I am perfectly indifferent, and shall make no demand of that nature on your father, since I am well aware that it could not be complied with, also that one thousand pounds in the four per cents which will not be yours till after your mother's decease, is all that you may ever be entitled to. On that head, therefore, I shall be uniformly silent; and you may be sure that no ungenerous reproach shall ever pass my lips when we are married.'*

WHEN WE ARE MARRIED! Poor Elizabeth sat trans-fixed somewhere between horror and hysteria as the juggernaut of Mr Collins' proposal lumbered on. Now, however, it is about to run her down. As Jane Austen notes with her unequalled gift for dry understatement, 'it was absolutely necessary to interrupt him now':

> *'You are too hasty, sir,' she cried. 'You forget I have made no answer. I am very sensible of the honour of your proposals, but it is impossible for me to do otherwise than to decline them . . .'*

'You must give me leave to flatter myself, my dear cousin,' replied Mr Collins, 'that your refusal of my addresses is merely words of course. It does not appear to me that my hand is unworthy of your acceptance, or that the establishment I can offer would be any other than highly desirable. Nor do I reckon the notice and kindness of Lady Catherine de Bourgh as the least of the advantages in my power to offer. As I must therefore conclude that you are not serious in your rejection of me, I shall choose to attribute it to your wish of increasing my love by suspense, according to the usual practice of elegant females. I am persuaded that when sanctioned by the express authority of both your excellent parents, my proposals will not fail of being acceptable.'

Nothing less than the row that ensues between Elizabeth's mother and her father, one violently for and the other as violently against Mr Collins, will do to give him the message that Elizabeth will not have him. But he shows the strength of his 'love' for her by bouncing smartly into the arms of a woman who will. Within three days the engagement is announced – between himself and Lady Catherine de Bourgh!

Have you ever thought that Jane Austen might have been exaggerating the pomposity and self-importance of Mr Collins? Then look at this real-life proposal from the same period. It was made in 1808 by an earnest young barrister with the unfortunate name of Thomas Trollope, to Fanny, the sister of his friend Henry Milton. Neither his hilarious handle, nor his ponderous approach, nor the shortness of their acquaintance (three months) prevented her from accepting him. The fact that she was then 28, in an era when the age of consent was 12 and many girls were old married women at 15, may have had something to do with it.

So could Miss Fanny have been pleased to receive this epistle?

MY DEAR MADAM,

   . . . *Is it most expedient for a man to make avowal of his attachment to a lady 'viva voce' ('anglice' in tête à tête) or by epistolary correspondence?*

   This preface explains the motive of my now addressing you. It will save me the necessity of a more explicit avowal, and declare to you that my future happiness on earth is at your disposal . . .

And so on, for pages and pages of pompous and prosaic guff. Mr Trollope, like Mr Collins, claims to despise those who 'contract alliances upon motives of a pecuniary nature', yet his letter goes into both his financial situation and hers in minute detail. Finally he winds up on a note of unconcious irony:

In doing this in the most simple manner, and in rejecting the flippant nonsense which I believe to be commonly used on occasions of this nature, I doubt not I have acted as well in conformity of your sentiments as those of, My Dear Madam,

   Your sincere admirer and devoted servant,

   THOS. ANTH. TROLLOPE

Romantic, no? Every line pounding with purple passion? Sadly, the ringing of the off-stage tills, which is the only music to be heard throughout this letter, was the tune to which poor Fanny had to dance all her life. Thos. Anth. proved a poor provider, Fanny a bonny breeder, and his thwarted expectations plus eight children brought the family low.

But it was as Fanny Trollope that she became something she could never have been as Miss Milton, a highly successful writer, traveller and lady of letters. She was famous as far afield as the USA, where her scourging of everything from American table manners to the slave trade brought the revolting natives out to riot in the streets. She also lived to enjoy the success of her even more famous son Anthony, the Barsetshire novelist. And even though superseded by him, Fanny could take comfort in one thought. There would always be one member of the family whose writing she could better – her husband's!

But of all the proposals of undesirable men, centre stage in the Theatre of Embarrassment must be the wretched heroine of Mary McCarthy's excruciating story, *The Man In The Brooks Brothers Shirt*. He is 'a pink, middle-aged stranger', a travelling salesman from Cleveland. She is a New Yorker, tripping West and desperately conscious of slumming; smart, yet not so street-smart that she can dodge the inevitable pass when it comes.

They meet on a long-distance Pullman at the start of a three-day journey. Her last memory is of drinking whisky with him in his compartment. When she wakes in the sleeping-berth the next morning, she realizes in a moment of toe-curling horror that *he is in there with her*, and naked . . .

> *Waves of shame began to run through her, like savage internal blushes, as fragments of the night before presented themselves for inspection . . . She had fought him off for a long time, but at length her will had softened. She had felt tired and kind, and thought 'why not?' Then there had been something peculiar about the love-making . . . There were (oh, Holy Virgin!) four-letter words that she had been forced to repeat, and, at the climax, a rain of blows on her buttocks that must surely (dear God!) have left bruises . . . If only nobody could know.*

Feverishly she tries to get dressed and leave without waking him. She is sick with disgust, and her feelings are vividly real. It seems like the most horripilating act of sexual congress you can imagine, as if King Kong had forced himself upon Fay Wray. Of course, he wakes up. She wants to go, but he won't let her:

> *The man seized her arms and pulled her down, sitting up himself beside her. He looked very fat, and the hairs on his chest were grey.*
>
> *'You can't go,' he said, quite simply and naturally, but as if he had been thinking about it all night long. 'I love you. I'm crazy about you. This is the most wonderful thing that has ever happened to me. You come to San Francisco with me and we'll go to Monterey, and I'll fix it with Leonie to get a divorce . . .'*
>
> *She stared at him incredulously, but there was no doubt of it: he was serious. He wanted to marry her. 'Kiss me,' he said, but she pulled away.*

And then in one short line she speaks for all the women who have ever suffered the attentions of selfish, brutal, stupid, repulsive, and above all self-satisfied men:

> *'I have to throw up,' she said.*

And she does!

Women Take Arms

> DOLLY LEVI: *Horace, you can't deny it, your wife would have to be a SOMEBODY. Answer me: am I a somebody?*
>
> VANDERGELDER: *You are . . . you are . . . A wonderful woman.*
>
> DOLLY LEVI: *Oh, you're partial.*
>
> VANDERGELDER: *Dolly, everybody knows that you could do anything you wanted to do*
>
> Thornton Wilder, *The Matchmaker*

WOMEN ARE NORMALLY THE RECIPIENTS, occasionally even the victims, of masculine marriage proposals. However not all the fair sex have been content to adopt the missionary position, to lie back and take whatever's coming. Some women are obliged to make the running themselves by virtue of their situation. British queens regnant, for instance, always have to propose. The idea is that no one of a lesser rank could presume to the impertinence.

This explains why Queen Victoria had to propose to Prince Albert. The whole thing threw her into an agony of apprehension, as she wrote to her uncle:

I may not have the FEELING for him which is requisite

to ensure happiness. I MAY like him as a friend, and as a COUSIN and as a BROTHER, but not more . . . I am very, VERY ANXIOUS . . .

The arrival of Prince Albert in person changed all this in the twinkling of an eye. 'Albert's *beauty* is *most striking*, and he so amiable and unaffected – in short, very *fascinating*,' the Queen confided. 'He seems *perfection*, and I think that I have the prospect of a very great happiness before me. I *love* him *more* than I can say.'

Head over heels, the little Queen lost no time. Within three days of his arrival, she sent for him to the Blue Closet at Windsor, and there, as she told her dear diary:

I said to him, that I thought he must be aware WHY I wished him to come here – and that it would make me TOO HAPPY if he would consent to what I wished (to marry me).

Albert broke into ecstatic German, kissed her hands, and accepted with joy. They were so happy together that, after Albert's death, Victoria could queen it no longer without him, but settled into her endless mourning as 'the Widow of Windsor'.

Most girls, though, propose to make sure of the man they love, or at least to try. In two of the world's greatest love stories, everyone always forgets that Juliet proposes to Romeo, and Scarlett O'Hara to Ashley Wilkes. Another impetus, for females, is the desire to protect themselves from all the other creepies and crawlies, ghosties and ghoulies, and things that want to go bump in the night.

Both factors influence the heroine of America's most famous marriage proposal in Longfellow's terrific poem, *The Courtship of Miles Standish*. The whole thing is a splendid piece of poetical prestidigitation anyway, since there *is* no courtship – and not exactly what you'd call a proposal, either. If that sounds ridiculous, now read on . . .

Miles Standish is a Founding Father, a great hero and war-leader in the early days of US colonial settlement. But he is grim, old and unattractive, both wrinkly and grizzly as a result of his martial life.

His friend John Alden is, by contrast, a pretty cute specimen of Early American Beefcake, 'fair-haired, azure-eyed, with a delicate Saxon complexion' (Robert Redford should play him in the film version). John also has a delicate Saxon reticence when it comes to women. He is nursing a manly passion for the lovely Priscilla, and can't breathe a word of it. Then he gets the thunderbolt revelation that grumpy old Miles Standish wants to make a Founding Mother out of her, and has delegated *him* to carry the offer!

> *Go to the damsel Priscilla,*
> *the loveliest maiden of Plymouth,*
> *Say that a blunt old Captain,*
> *a man not of words but of actions,*
> *Offers his hand and his heart,*
> *the hand and the heart of a soldier . . .*

Sounds terrific, no? the proposal you always wanted? Shame on you, where's your sense of 'my country, 'tis of thee . . .'?

To John's further confusion, the great warrior confesses:

> *I can march up to a fortress,*
> *and summon the place to surrender,*
> *But march up to a woman,*
> *with such a proposal I dare not.*
> *I am not afraid of bullets,*
> *nor shot from the mouth of a cannon,*

> *But of a thundering 'No!'*
>   *point-blank from the mouth of a woman,*
> *That I confess I'm afraid of . . .*

So there's no getting out of it. With a heavy heart John makes his way to Priscilla, and gets down to his task: 'I have come to you now, with an offer and proffer of marriage'. And offer and proffer he does, stumbling his way through this strange proxy proposal.

Understandably, Priscilla is not impressed. She floors the proposer with one practical question: 'Why does he not come himself, and take the trouble to woo me?' John's attempts to get his bat to this googly get him into an even deeper mess. Finally the exasperated Priscilla gives him a man-sized nudge in one of the immortal lines of American literature:

Why don't you speak for yourself, John?

And she gets him in the end. But not all women are as good judges of husband material as Priscilla. Both Americans and British know the larky ballad, 'Oh soldier, soldier, will you marry me, with your musket, fife and drum?' In this song the girl has obviously fallen hook, line and sinker for what you might call the soldier's outward parts. Oh yes. Oh, soldier. You know what she means. There *is* something about a soldier – preferably a Heavy Dragoon. Thomas Hardy certainly knew what he was doing in *Far From The Madding Crowd*, when he put Sergeant Troy in the dashing brigade of the 11th Hussars, and made him bewitch the heroine with his . . . what's the word? . . . *swordsmanship* . . .

The soldier in the ballad is just such another lady-killer and jack-go-nimble as Sergeant Troy. Although there are as many variants of the song as voices to sing them, in all the versions he successively extracts from the besotted maid a complete new wardrobe, down to hat, sock and boots, as the price for marrying her, and then delivers the *coup de grâce*:

> *Oh no, sweet maid, I cannot marry you,*
> *For I have a wife and children, too —*
> *For I've got me a wife at home.*

Filthy swine, as my father would have said. And the pater finds plenty of support for his view in both history and literature. The woman betrayed is a very common theme, while never less than heartbreaking. W. H. Auden updated it with a modern inflection in his poem *Johnny*:

> *O but he was as fair as a garden in flower,*
> *As slender and tall as the great Eiffel tower,*
> *When the waltz throbbed out on the long promenade*
> *His eyes and his smile they went straight to my heart;*
> *'O marry me, Johnny — I'll love and obey':*
> *But he frowned like thunder and he went away.*

The truly modern woman, however, does not just timidly bleat 'marry me', with a great big question mark. As imagined by the irreplaceable Joe Orton in his black comedy, *Loot*, she moves swiftly in on the kill, then goes for the jugular with the grace of a panther.

Fay has been the resident nurse during the last illness of McLeavy's wife:

FAY: *You've been a widower for three days. Have you considered a second marriage yet?*

MCLEAVY: *A second wife would be a physical impossibility.*

FAY: *I'll hear none of that. My last husband at sixty came through with flying colours. Three days after our*

> *wedding he was performing extraordinary feats . . .*
> *You must marry a girl with youth and vitality. I can*
> *visualize her — medium height, slim, fair hair. A*
> *regular visitor to some place of worship. And an ex-*
> *member of the League of Mary.*

MCLEAVY: *Someone like yourself?*

FAY: *Exactly.*

Meanwhile the late Mrs McLeavy lies downstage left in her coffin, awaiting the attentions of the undertaker and his henchmen. As Fay presses on with her plan, it's plain to see why Orton was dubbed 'the Oscar Wilde of welfare state gentility'. Mrs McLeavy has left all her money to Fay. McLeavy, now dispossessed as well as bereaved, objects:

MCLEAVY: *Couldn't you just give it to me?*

FAY: *Think of the scandal.*

MCLEAVY: *What do you suggest, then?*

FAY: *We must have a joint bank account.*

MCLEAVY: *Wouldn't that cause an even bigger scandal?*

FAY: *Not if we were married.*

MCLEAVY: *Married? But then you'd have my money as well as Mrs McLeavy's.*

FAY: *That's one way of looking at it.*

MCLEAVY: *No. I'm too old. My health wouldn't stand up to a young wife.*

FAY: *I'm a qualified nurse.*

MCLEAVY: *You'd have to give up your career.*

FAY: *I'd do it for you.*

MCLEAVY: *I can give you nothing in return.*

FAY: *I ask for nothing. I'm a woman. Only half the human race can say that without fear of contradiction. Go ahead. Ask me to marry you. I've no intention of*

♡ 68 ♡

refusing. On your knees. I'm a great believer in traditional positions.

MCLEAVY: *The pains in my legs.*

FAY: *Exercise is good for them. Use any form of proposal you like. Try to avoid abstract nouns.*

MCLEAVY: *Mrs McLeavy is keeping her Maker waiting. I'll pay my addresses to you after the interment.*

The echoes of Oscar Wilde heard here continue to sound throughout the rest of the play, where a flurry of proposals and counter-proposals ensues before the situation is resolved. Joe Orton was no mere imitator. How close he came to the exchanges of real life is demonstrated by a tangy extract from Joan Collins' raunchy autobiography, *Past Imperfect*. Here she describes her success in proposing to the film magnate Arthur Loewe Jr:

The gossip columnists had started hinting that we were on the verge of matrimony — well, why not? It seemed like a good idea at the time. I broached the subject . . .

'. . . if you don't want me to date other guys, we ought to get engaged or something.'

'Engaged!' he looked flabbergasted. 'You've only been divorced five minutes. You've been saying for a year that you don't EVER want to get married again, so why do you want to get engaged, for Christ's sake?'

'Don't you want to?' I said calmly, lighting a Pall Mall and blowing furious smoke rings.

'It isn't that I don't want to, Babee,' he slumped beside me and entwined his long bony fingers in mine. 'I just don't know if I can be faithful to you for that length of time.'

I looked at him with growing consternation. 'You mean you want to fuck around?'

'Spoken like the Queen of England,' he said drily . . .

Joan didn't get her man this time. But after she won the serious movie role of a tormented novice in *Sea Wife*, and he satirically rechristened the film *I Fucked A Nun*, she went off the idea anyway!

Well, only some marriages are made in heaven. The others need a fair bit of terrestrial stage management to get them off the ground. This is the story of Maggie and Willie in an evergreen drama, *Hobson's Choice*. Maggie, at thirty, is the unmarried daughter of the bootmaker Henry Hobson. She has been working like a dog for her father all her life, and her prospects are getting dimmer rather than brighter.

Maggie develops a fellow-feeling for Willie, her father's downtrodden labourer, who is nevertheless 'a genius at making boots'. She forms a plan in her mind — but then she has to break it to Willie:

MAGGIE: *We're a pair, Will Mossop.*
WILLIE: *You're a wonder in the shop, Miss Maggie.*
MAGGIE: *And you're a marvel in the workshop. Well?*
WILLIE: *Well what?*
MAGGIE: *It seems to me to point one way.*
WILLIE: *What way is that?*
MAGGIE: *You're leaving me to do the work, my lad . . .*
          I've watched you for a long time, and everything I've
          seen, I've liked. I think you'll do for me.
WILLIE: *What way, Miss Maggie?*

The innocent Willie has no idea what's going on. Beneath her brisk Northern exterior, Maggie is revealing both her true feelings for him, and her scheme for their future life together in a domestic and business partnership:

WILLIE: *What dost want me for?*
MAGGIE: *To invest in. You're a business idea in the*
          shape of a man.

♡ 70 ♡

WILLIE: *Partnership! Oh that's a different thing. I thought you were axing me to wed you.*

MAGGIE: *I am.*

WILLIE: *Well, by gum! And you the master's daughter!*

MAGGIE: *I'll tell you something, Will. It's a poor sort of woman who'll stay lazy when she sees her best chance slipping from her.*

WILLIE: *I'm your best chance?*

MAGGIE: *You are that, Will . . . I want your hand in mine and your word for it that you'll go through life with me for the best we can get out of it.*

Maggie may be only a Salford lass, but that's as good a proposal as many a better-educated man has ever made. And like a man, she has to beat down some nervous hesitation on the part of her intended, especially his terror of her tyrannical father.

But comically enough, it is old Hobson who brings out the man in Willie, and throws them into each other's arms, when he tries to take his belt to Willie and 'leather the love out of him':

WILLIE: *I've nobbut one answer for you. Maggie, I've none kissed you yet. I shirked before. But by gum, I'll kiss you now*

HE KISSES HER

and take you and hold you. And if Mr Hobson raises that strap again, I'll do more. I'll walk straight out of the shop with thee and us two 'ull set up for ourselves.

MAGGIE: *Willie! I knew you had it in you, lad!*

This is only the first of many kisses that they enjoy together – and success in their business as well!

Man's the hunter, woman's the hunted, so the tradition goes. But sometimes the hunters declare a close season when there's no reason why the sport shouldn't be enjoyed all the year round. So if you're feeling a bit un-hunted, reverse the roles. Borrow a trick or two from any of the women above, stalk your gentleman quarry, and when you've got him in your sights — propose!

10

Come Fly With Me

Now while the dark about our loves is strewn,
Light of my dark, blood of my heart, O come!
And night will catch her breath up and be dumb.

Leave thy father, leave thy mother,
And thy brother . . .

Francis Thompson, *Arab Love Song*

MANY A BRAVE DOE HAS secured her buck by daring to make the 'one great leap in the dark' at the right moment. And among themselves women are rarely coy about these things. A very refined elderly lady was once showing me round a perfect English garden, and pointed out an unusual border plant of a throbbing red-purple habit, as gardeners say. 'It's called "Marry Me Quick!",' she said, looking me straight in the eye, 'you can see why.'

Most of us are still old-fashioned enough to want our buck (or bull, or stallion, lion, tiger, pussy-cat or elephant) to leap on *us*, to demonstrate his uncontrollable passion and carry us away. ' 'E throwed her acrorse the pummel of 'is saddle and bored 'er orf to his tent like the Shriek of Araby,' is the way this classic female fantasy was summed up once by an old Cockney lady who had seen *all* the silent movies.

What women want (are you listening, Freud?) is a man who is not afraid to love – they can do without the sheikly trappings of tent, horse and pummel, especially the latter! The ideal hero rises naturally to the grand romantic gesture, and the greatest of these is the proposal that 'sweeps you right orf your feet' in the words of my Cockney authority.

It's axiomatic, of course, that he's not supposed to be sweeping you under the carpet, or straight into some bin or other. You want him to carry you into a life that you have dreamed of, yet never dared to hope for. The ideal proposal comes as a liberation for a female – the only kind of women's liberation that m and f are likely to agree on.

The Proposal as Liberation has a long and distinguished pedigree. In its essence, it is the Cinderella story – the poor girl, the 'some day my prince will come' fantasy, and he *does*. This is the basic formula for all romance fiction, in any language, any day or age. Only the hostile forces which the girl is dying to be liberated from vary considerably according to the circumstances.

Often the heroine is battling alone against high odds. She has to endure the loss of a beloved parent, desperate money worries, a tangled web of others' deception, and even the friendly neighbourhood sex maniac thrown in. Like the dark and distracting Zeb in Jessica Steele's *Price To Be Met*, the hero offers not only marriage, but release from all this, with financial and emotional security thrown in at a high level, too:

> '*You are going to marry me, aren't you?*' *he asked . . .*
> '*all I need to know is that you love me. If you want a fur coat I'll give you a hundred, but you've got to love me, got to marry me.*'

♡ 74 ♡

Modest Proposals

'Zeb, Zeb, I do, I will — you've no idea of the agonies I've been through . . .'

'Oh my darling, darling girl! To think you've been through all that, all the mental anguish and suffering you've been through — some of it at my hands, too . . .' He broke off as if his thoughts were almost too much for him to take. Then with a gentleness that was almost a benediction, he tenderly kissed her eyes, transferring his warm mouth to her lips. 'I shall make it all up to you,' he said. 'Never again will you know such terrible anxiety.'

Jessica Steele is one of the writers for the great romance house of Mills and Boon, publishers of, in their own modest phrase, 'books that please'. In fact their publications give their women readers so much more than pleasure. They're a magic carpet to a better world than this, where love is all in all and men are as dashing, kind and sexy as women want them to be (now sexy's another thing, Sigmund . . .)

The reigning queen of romance writing, unchallenged and unchallengeable, is Barbara Cartland, usually photographed in gorgeous glittery frocks, snow-white mink or fox fur, and bedecked in the small truck-load of jewels appropriate to her position. She has displayed her versatility as a writer in over three hundred books, of biography, social commentary and drama in addition to her novels; people forget how hard she has worked all her life. But her real fame and enormous popularity rest on her love stories, which all end, as we hope they will, in proposals of marriage.

All this is drawn directly from Barbara Cartland's own experiences. As she told the *Daily Mail*:

No young man ever suggested anything to me but a wedding ring. They were emotional, violent in their protestations of

♡ 75 ♡

*love, and three men swore they would kill themselves if I
wouldn't marry them. But I was untouched, adored,
worshipped and wooed.*

There aren't many women who can say that. But there
aren't many women who haven't wanted to. Barbara
Cartland appeals to the instinct of romance in every female
soul. And as the favourite author of the Princess of Wales,
she can even claim to have been a guiding light in the
most famous real-life romance of the century!

The hero's proposal to the heroine is the climax of the
love story. It's always different, yet always familiar, and
keenly expected by the reader, if not by the recipient. For
there is the element of surprise to consider. The proposal
takes the unsuspecting heroine quite unaware. She simply
had not dared to hope — and it comes to her like a divine
revelation:

> *'Tell me, Syringa,' said the Earl after a moment, 'do you
> remember why my mother gave this brooch to me?'*
>
> *'Yes of course,' Syringa replied, 'she gave it to you for
> your wife.'*
>
> *'And that is why,' the Earl said very quietly, 'I am
> asking you now, Syringa, to accept it as — a gift.'*
>
> *It seemed to Syringa that her heart stood still. Then in
> a small frightened voice she said:*
>
> *'I do not think I . . . understand what you are . . .
> saying.'*
>
> *'I will try to make it clearer,' the Earl answered. 'I love
> you, my darling, and I want more than I have ever wanted
> anything in my life, that you should marry me.'*

This is the proposal of *The Ruthless Rake*, who adds to the
attractions of his earldom, fortune and estate that spice of
wickedness that makes men so irresistible. He takes his

place in the Cartland heroes' gallery alongside such other deliciously attractive rogues as:

The Wicked Marquis
The Dangerous Dandy
The Bored Bridegroom
and
The Penniless Peer

Now they really don't make men like that any more! It's a consolation that they're still writing stories about men like that, given the contemporary shortage of The Thing Itself.

For these stories continue a long and honourable tradition which goes all the way back to the Middle Ages. It was in twelfth-century France, in some sun-baked royal courtyard of Provence, that women and men too first sighed over tales of the triumph of love. Since then there have been some memorable titles to keep the torch alight. One of the most famous and potent was Mrs Henry Wood's runaway Victorian bestseller, *East Lynne*.

Like all the queens of romance fiction, Mrs Henry Wood has been sneered at and mocked, but she can afford to have the last laugh on her critics. *East Lynne* was not only an overnight sensation as a novel. Made into a play, it swept the London stage and held the boards for years. Whenever a high-class super-weepie, with bags of action and a rattling good story was called for, *East Lynne* came down off the shelf and turned up trumps.

Now admittedly the story is not strong on probability, starting with the tragic death of the heroine's father. He goes off with a form of gout unknown to medical science, which flies to his stomach and then attacks his heart. Even more of a strain on the willing suspension of disbelief is the situation in which the heroine returns from a train crash, disfigured and disguised, to take up residence again under her husband's roof – and neither he nor her children realize that it's her! This of course is the origin of the immortal line:

Dead! And never called me mother!

But anyone who reads the gripping account of the Lady Isabel Vane will forgive Mrs Henry anything. She has you in her grasp from her heroine's first entrance, with her vivid picture of:

a light, graceful, girlish form, a face of surpassing beauty, beauty that is rarely seen, save from the imagination of a painter, dark shining curls falling on her neck and shoulders smooth as a child's, fair delicate arms decorated with pearls, and a flowing dress of costly white lace . . .

Naturally the Lady Isabel is not just a pretty face; 'she was as good as she was beautiful', insists Mrs H. The author really makes us care about the heroine as she puts her through the most dreadful and ingenious trials. After the death of her father, the ancestral home of East Lynne is sold about her ears. It is under these wretched circumstances that she receives a surprise visit from the gentleman who has bought East Lynne. She confides in him how much she misses her father and her home:

Would I could awake and find the last few months but a hideous dream! – that I could find my dear father alive again! that we were still living peacefully at East Lynne! It would be a very Eden to me now!

This plaintive appeal cuts to the heart of the listener, Archibald Carlyle. The irresistible impulse comes upon him to free her from her troubles and restore her to her rightful place:

What was Mr Carlyle about to say? What emotion was it that agitated his countenance, impeded his breath, and dyed his face blood red?

'There is but one way,' he began, taking her hand and nervously playing with it, 'only one way in which you could return to East Lynne. And that way — I may not presume, perhaps, to point it out.'

She looked at him, and waited for an explanation.

'If my words offend you, Lady Isabel, check them as their presumption deserves, and forgive me. May I — dare I — offer you to return to East Lynne as its mistress?'

She did not comprehend him in the slightest degree; the drift of his meaning never dawned on her. 'Return to East Lynne as its mistress?' she repeated in bewilderment.

'And as my wife.'

And then what? Does she, or doesn't she? Mrs H keeps you on the edge of your seat from beginning to end; when, if you aren't on your third box of Kleenex, you must have missed out on the standard issue of tear ducts. It's terribly sad, harrowing in fact. If you have tears, go grab a copy of this high-pitched, super-duper tale of loss and desolation and prepare to shed them *all*.

Interestingly, women are not the only ones who find that a proposal of marriage may be the liberation longed for from drudgery and disappointment. In one of F. Scott Fitzgerald's jewel-like short stories *The Sensible Thing*, George O'Kelly is frantically trying to secure, by long distance, the hand of a 'dear little girl' in Tennessee. Toiling unhappily as an insurance clerk in New York at $40 a week, George reaches breaking point when his girl writes that she is reconsidering their understanding. In a frenzy of telegraphese George blasts off his proposal, with consequences as yet unforeseen:

♡ 79 ♡

LETTER DEPRESSED ME HAVE YOU LOST
YOUR NERVE YOU ARE FOOLISH AND JUST
UPSET TO THINK OF BREAKING OFF WHY
NOT MARRY ME IMMEDIATELY SURE WE
CAN MAKE IT ALL RIGHT –

*He hesitated for a wild minute, and then added in a
hand that could scarcely be recognized as his own,* IN
ANY CASE I WILL ARRIVE TOMORROW AT SIX
O'CLOCK.

Having sent this offer of his hand and heart winging off
down the wires all the way south-west, George has to turn
his mind to practicalities. In his impetuosity he has not
accounted for more mundane considerations, like going to
work – a true romantic does not stop to calculate at
moments of crisis. George's proposal turns out to be a
point of departure in his life, in more senses than one:

> *George O'Kelly reached the insurance office at his usual run
> and went straight to the manager's office.*
> *'I want to get four days' vacation.'*
> *'Where'd you go last time? To your home?'*
> *'No, I went to – a place in Tennessee.'*
> *'Well, where do you want to go this time?'*
> *'Well, this time I want to go to – a place in Tennessee.'*
> *'You're consistent, anyhow,' said the manager drily.*
> *'But I didn't realize you were employed here as a travelling
> salesman.'*
> *'I'm not!' cried George desperately, 'but I've got to go.'*
> *'Alright,' agreed Mr Chambers, 'but you don't have to
> come back, so don't!'*

To his total stupefaction, George is fired. Yet somehow,
this is not bad news:

> *To his own astonishment as well as Mr Chambers',*

George's face grew pink with pleasure. He felt happy, exultant — for the first time in six months he was absolutely free. Tears of gratitude stood in his eyes and he seized Mr Chambers warmly by the hand.

'I want to thank you,' he said with a rush of emotion. 'I don't want to come back. Only I couldn't quit for myself, you see, and I want to thank you for — for quitting for me.'

He waved his hand magnanimously, shouted aloud, 'You owe me three days' salary, but you can keep it,' and rushed from the office. Mr Chambers rang for his stenographer to ask if Mr O'Kelly had seemed queer lately. He had fired many men in the course of his career, and they had taken it in many different ways, but none of them had thanked him — ever before.

George's proposal proves to be a true liberation. Freed from a job he loathes, he gets everything he ever wanted, including of course his girl, exactly how it happened for Fitzgerald himself in real life.

Everyone, whether male or female, cherishes the idea of the magical proposal that will give entry to the life desired. And it isn't pure fantasy, the dream that only comes true in fairy stories and Barbara Cartland. It can happen in real life. It happened for the Prince and Princess of Wales, who found it, in their own words, 'unbelievable' and 'pretty amazing'. And it happened, on a rather different level, to my father's eldest sister, Aunt Lillie.

Aunt Lillie's girlhood had been blighted by loving and losing a man she had met out riding — 'he was in the Cavalry', the family said, to explain away the fatal attraction. For virtually the next twenty years she loitered palely through the parlour half-life of the sheltered young female. She attended her mother on visits to other ladies, she went to church, she pressed flowers and she did her embroidery.

Then, when she was forty, Lillie met a captain in the navy. They fell in love, he proposed, and flushed with joy Lillie announced her engagement to the family, of which my father was the only other genuine human specimen. Nothing could equal the family's sense of shock and outrage. It was unseemly, unthinkable. It had better stop.

Only my mother, famous for her gentle touch, thought to ask Lillie how she felt. 'It's passion, Lucy, *passion*!' cried Lillie, rapturously. This gave her the strength she needed. She went on to marry the captain, and so escaped the clutches of a life-denying family and the miseries of a loveless existence. And they lived happily together with each other and a little dog for the rest of their days.

Some women, of course, have far higher expectations of marriage than this, and far more brilliant vistas of the life desired. But they still expect that the Ideal Man will provide it. In a comical exchange from a famous play of 1707, *The Beaux' Stratagem*, two Restoration belles compare the behaviour of their lovers:

DORINDA: *My lover was on his knees to me.*
MRS SULLEN: *And mine was on his tiptoes to me.*
DORINDA: *Mine vowed to die for me.*
MRS SULLEN: *Mine swore to die with me.*
DORINDA: *Mine swore the softest, most moving things.*
MRS SULLEN: *Mine had his moving things, too.*
DORINDA: *Mine kissed my hand ten thousand times.*
MRS SULLEN: *Mine has all that pleasure to come.*
DORINDA: *Mine offered marriage.*
MRS SULLEN: *O Lord! D'ye call that a moving thing?*

Mrs Sullen does not regard a proposal as something to be pleased about. She is already married, and unhappily. But

Dorinda, the heroine, feels sure that she can find the man who will not only love her, but deliver her into the glittering society where she will be truly at home:

> DORINDA: *His offer of marriage is the sharpest arrow in his quiver, my dear! If I marry my Lord Aimwell, there will be title, place, and precedence, the Park, the play and the drawing-room, splendour, equipage, noise and flambeaux. – 'Hey, my Lady Aimwell's servants there!' – 'Lights, lights to the stairs!' – 'My Lady Aimwell's coach forward!' – 'Stand by, make room for her ladyship!' Are not these things moving?'*

You betcha booties they are, as Bette Midler says. The nearest I ever got to a title was once in New York, when in the confusion of the moment a judge introduced me to an entire courtful of hard-bitten New Yorkers, including the defendant, as Her Honour Judge Lady Miles. No one but me was impressed. New Yorkers don't impress so easily, and the defendant, looking down the barrel of a long jail sentence, had other things on his mind. But suddenly in that moment, I had a vision of how it could be . . .

Not only how it could be, but how it should be, is the way it is in one of the most magical and haunting romances ever written. Daphne du Maurier's ever-green *Rebecca* goes from strength to strength, conquering each new generation as soon as it gets old enough to read a book or see a movie – for both versions are equally memorable in their own way.

But nobody who has seen the superb 1939 film can ever think of the gauche heroine and her brooding lover with any other faces than those of Joan Fontaine and Laurence Olivier. Olivier is at his best in the proposal sequence, which shows off his gift for sardonic, throwaway playing. He is exquisitely partnered by Fontaine as the shy exschoolgirl, miserably drudging as a companion to selfish, ill-tempered Mrs Van Hopper, who finds to her horror that she is about to be rushed off to New York.

For she has only just met Maxim de Winter, the handsome, rich and mysterious owner of the legendary mansion, Manderley. She rushes to him to make her last goodbye, and finds him unmoved and enigmatic:

> *'Which would you prefer, New York or Manderley? You can take your choice.'*
>
> *'Don't make a joke about it; it's unfair,' I said. 'I think I had better see about those tickets, and say goodbye now.'*
>
> *'I repeat, the choice is open to you. Either you go to America with Mrs Van Hopper, or you come home to Manderley with me.'*
>
> *'Do you mean you want a secretary or something?'*
>
> *'No, I'm asking you to marry me, you little fool.'*

This classic moment is just as unexpected in the movie as in the book. The director, none other than Hitchcock, has screwed the tension up so tight, with the clock ticking the time away, the phone ringing in the empty apartment, and the harpy employer screeching to be gone. Then there is Fontaine in that unrepeatable trilby being quizzed by Olivier, scrumptious as ever despite being caught in his vest with a smear of shaving cream like a duelling scar on his left cheek.

And as in all high romance, the heroine cannot believe that it is happening for her:

> *I watched a fly settle on the marmalade, and he brushed it away impatiently.*
>
> *'You haven't answered my question. Are you going to marry me?'*

This sudden talk of marriage bewildered me, even shocked me I think. It was as if the King had asked me. It did not ring true. And he went on eating his marmalade as if everything were natural. In books men knelt to women, and it would be moonlight. Not at breakfast, not like this.

'My suggestion doesn't seem to have gone too well,' he said. 'I'm sorry. I rather thought you loved me. A fine blow to my conceit.'

'I do love you,' I said. 'I love you dreadfully. You've made me very unhappy, and I've been crying all night because I thought I should never see you again.'

But slowly, slowly the realization grows and flowers in her mind, bursts into a thousand shooting stars:

And suddenly I realized that it would all happen; I would be his wife . . . Mrs de Winter. I would be Mrs de Winter. I saw the polished table in the dining room and the long candles. Maxim sitting at the end. A party of twenty-four. I had a flower in my hair. Everyone looked towards me, holding up his glass. 'We must drink the health of the bride,' and Maxim saying afterwards, 'I have never seen you look so lovely.' Great cool rooms, filled with flowers. My bedroom with a fire in the winter, someone knocking at the door. And a woman comes in smiling; she is Maxim's sister, and she is saying, 'It's really wonderful how happy you have made him; everyone is so pleased, you are such a success.' Mrs de Winter. I would be Mrs de Winter.

And she is.

Some people, especially men, scoff at the great romanciers, and those who enjoy their work. But 'you got to have a dream', as the wise old woman in *South Pacific* reminds us, 'if you don't have a dream, how you gonna have a dream come true?'

No woman should be made to feel ashamed of enjoying tales of love and fulfilment, of dreaming of the lover and the marriage that sets her free from worldly cares to fly to the heights. And where is the man mean enough to admit that he is too poor-spirited, too base-hearted to rise to the level of a woman's highest hopes? For romance stories are just these emotions and aspirations writ large — and as such they are a treasure-house of the finest impulses of the human heart.

The Tender Trap

You see a pair of laughing eyes,
And suddenly you're sighing sighs,
You think there's something wrong,
You string along,
And then — snap!
Those eyes, those sighs, they're part of the tender trap.

Sammy Cahn and Jimmy Van Heussen

A PROPOSAL IS A PARADOX — just as it can be the liberation of a woman, it can also be the clanging of the trap door for a man. The state matrimonial has not always had a good press. Marriage is an institution, said Oscar Wilde, and who wants to live in an institution? His view received some support from Ogden Nash in a wry poem called *I Do, I Will, I Have*:

Just as I am unsure of the difference
  between flora and fauna and flotsam and jetsam,
I am quite sure that marriage is an alliance of two people
  one of whom never remembers birthdays
  and the other never forgetsam,
And he refuses to believe there is a leak in the water pipe
  or the gas pipe and she is convinced
  she is about to asphyxiate or drown,

And she says, Quick get up and get my hairbrushes off
  the windowsill, it's raining in and he replies
  Oh they're all right, it's only raining straight down.
That is why marriage is so much more interesting than
  divorce,
Because it's the only known example of the happy meeting of
  the immovable object and the irresistible force.

In the past, men were often deliberately trapped by those who believed that as marriage was an inescapable social duty, a man might as well get on with it as soon as possible. Marriage was not seen as a romantic exchange between two people in private — it was a business, a very serious business, and in some cases an industry.

Among those at the mass-market end of the marriage trade are the Reverend and Mrs Allaby, who have no less than seven daughters to get off in Samuel Butler's sardonic critique of Victorian hypocrisy, *The Way Of All Flesh*. As the mother of the seven disposables, Mrs Allaby is a keen proponent of Austen's Law,[1] and tireless in her pursuit of any available single male.

A prime victim is Theobald, a hapless young curate who is drawn into the family circle, fussed over and buttered up. But who is to have him? At the cynical suggestion of their father, the girls play cards, with the prospective husband as the stake. Theobald is then manoeuvred into proposing to the winner, Miss Christina. But he is really unsure about the whole thing, and his reluctance comes through in his letter of declaration — he solicits rejection in every line:

1. 'It is a truth universally acknowledged, that a single man in possession of a good fortune, must be in want of a wife' — *Pride and Prejudice*.

DEAREST MISS CHRISTINA,

I do not know whether you have guessed the feelings that I have long entertained for you — feelings which I have concealed as much as I could for fear of drawing you into an engagement which, if you enter into it, must be prolonged for a considerable time; but however this may be, it is out of my power to conceal them longer; I love you, ardently, devotedly, and send these few lines asking you to be my wife because I dare not trust my tongue to give adequate expression to the magnitude of my affection for you . . .

I ought to warn you that in the event of your consenting to be my wife, it may be years before our union can be consummated, for I cannot marry until a college living is offered to me. If you see fit to reject me, I shall be grieved rather than surprised —

Ever most devotedly yours,

THEOBALD PONTIFEX

Theobald is pleased with this. He has at least tried to sound like a lover. Even more pleased is Christina, who accepts him prontissimo, and eventually the pair marry, to live as happily as can be expected under the circumstances.

But often when a man makes an ill-considered plunge into wedlock, it is more a question of his falling than being pushed. Such is the case of H. G. Wells's hero in *The History of Mr Polly*. Vague feelings of dissatisfaction with his life, ambitions to open a shop, a sunny afternoon in the park and the presence of a girl he has been seeing for some time, all come together in one fatal impulse:

'One did ought to be happy in a shop,' said Miriam, with a note of unusual softness in her voice . . .

'I could be happy in a shop,' he said.

His sense of effect had made him pause.

♡ 89 ♡

'If I had the right company,' he added.

She became very still . . . He stopped, and felt falling, falling, through the aching silence that followed . . .

'You don't mean you've got someone —?'

He found himself plunging.

'I've got someone in my eye this minute,' he said.

'Elfrid!' she said, turning to him. 'You don't mean —' Well, DID he mean? 'I do!' he said.

'Not reely!' she clinched her hands to keep still. He took the conclusive step. 'Well, you and me, Miriam, in a little shop, with a cat and a canary' — he tried too late to get back to a hypothetical note. 'Just suppose it!'

'You mean,' said Miriam, 'you're in love with me, Elfrid?' What possible answer can a man give to such a question, but 'Yes'?

So Mr Polly's sense of gallantry in part contributes to his undoing. Miriam is troubled with no such refinement of scruple. She claps hold of the stunned Polly, and seals the bargain with the first 'reel' kiss he has been granted. This is the only part of the process that Mr Polly can rumble the attraction of, for it is not a happy moment.

He had a curious feeling that it would be very satisfying to marry and have a wife — only somehow he wished it wasn't Miriam . . . For the life of him Mr Polly could not tell whether he was full of tender anticipation or regretful panic . . .

She rose and made as if to take Mr Polly's arm. But Mr Polly felt that their condition must be nakedly exposed to the ridicule of the world by such a linking, and evaded her movement . . . a flood of hesitation and terrors seized him.

'Don't tell anyone yet a bit,' he said.

'Only Mother,' said Miriam firmly.

As in the marriage of Christina and Theobald, the mother
is a formidable stage-manager and even director of these
proceedings. But a young couple can trap themselves
without any outside assistance, as the Fun Boy Three sing
in 'Tunnel of Love':

> *There are twenty-two catches when you strike your matches,*
> *Get down on your knees in the tunnel of love.*

> > *The tunnel of love,*
> > *You fall in feet first,*
> > *In the tunnel of love,*
> > *You think of yourselves*
> > *As really good friends*
> > *But you know how it always ends*
> > *In the tunnel of love.*
> > *So you get engaged and have a party*
> > *Only seventeen when the wedding bells chime,*
> > *Got a room with a view and a kid on the way,*
> > *Hope you make it to the church on time . . .*

This is exactly the situation of the young couple in Stan
Barstow's *A Kind of Loving*. The hero, Vic, is a rebel
without a rebellion, James Dean northern-style (failed).
He has been having sex with Ingrid, almost absent-
mindedly towards the end, on the Everest principle,
because she's there. And you'll never guess what . . .

> *I know she's pregnant. I know for sure. I know for sure I'm*
> *not going to get out of this one. I'm caught and that's a*
> *fact. Capital F-a-c-t. This is where all the dreams end,*
> *Vic Brown. No need to go on looking for that girl. You've*
> *found her, the only one you'll get now. You're trapped and*
> *there's no way out. Oh, what a fool, what a bloody, bloody*
> *fool!*

♡ 91 ♡

> *So that's it. It only wants saying, and I lean my head against the roof post and look out over the park and say it.*
>
> *'Don't worry. We'll get married. That's what we'll do.'*
>
> *She says nothing and in a few seconds I hear a little noise and I turn round and see she's crying.*

In this sad moment, the fate of the couple is sealed. We can see ahead for them vistas of a lifetime of nappies, bills and rows, first the overcrowded house and then the empty nest. But Vic can think only of himself, and Ingrid's tears provoke him to another spasm of disgust:

> *She's sobbing away like billy-ho now. The hanky's out and the waterworks are turned on good and proper.*
>
> *'I've always wanted to marry you, Vic,' she says. 'I've often imagined how you might propose to me. And now it has to be this way. Forcing you into it . . . You've no need to if you don't want to,' she says all at once. 'I shan't force you.'*
>
> *This is a laugh. Even if she won't force me, what about everybody else? I can just imagine them if I make so much as a sign that I don't want to go through with it. I can just see them all putting the screws on. It'd take a better man than me to stand out against all that . . .*
>
> *And as I'm standing there I wish to God, I wish more than I've ever wished for anything else, that I'd never laid eyes on her.*

Ingrid's distress, however callously disregarded by Vic, is a moving reminder that the trap when sprung closes on two people, and not on the mighty male member alone. Shotgun or even ·22, weddings are in fact worse on the female, since she's the one to be lumbered with all the work and worry of child-bearing, while being also denied the release of getting out of the house, having a job, seeing a few mates.

The wrong man at the wrong time ruins a woman's life. But perhaps it takes one of the most powerful of modern women writers to drive home this point:

> *Like a satiated nursling, he let the nipple pop out of his mouth, formed a kiss of boundless love and gratitude against the side of her breast, and lay utterly still except for the heaves of his breathing. He could feel her mouth in his hair, her hand down inside his shirt, and suddenly he seemed to recollect himself, opened his eyes. Briskly he sat up, pulled her slip straps up her arms, then her dress, and fastened all the buttons deftly.*
>
> *'You'd better marry me, Meghann,' he said, eyes soft and laughing. 'I don't think your brothers would approve one bit of what we just did.'*
>
> *'Yes, I think I'd better, too,' she agreed, lids lowered, a delicate flush on her cheeks.*
>
> *'Let's tell them tomorrow morning.'*
>
> *'Why not? The sooner the better.'*
>
> *'Next Saturday I'll drive you into Gilly. We'll see Father Thomas — I suppose you'd like a church wedding — arrange for the banns, and buy an engagement ring.'*
>
> *'Thank you, Luke.'*

This is, of course, one of many climactic moments in Colleen McCullough's world-sweeping epic, *The Thorn Birds*. One thing that makes this book a mega-experience is that McCullough never pulls back from the painful, tragic and disastrous elements of life. She doesn't feel the usual compulsion to make it all come right in the last reel, and she tells it hard and strong from the woman's point of view.

♥ 93 ♥

Here Meghann, a complete novice in life and sex, has dropped into the hands of Luke, whose obsessional selfishness and limited mentality only become fully clear to her over the years of their life together. The sexual act which compromises her Catholic conscience into marriage is no more than the nipple-nuzzling described above. But she is 'convinced he had done to her that thing which made babies start'.

Yet green as Meggie is, she knows more of the flesh and the devil than anyone around her guesses. She has had her own baptism in the flames of love and desire, so intense that she never recovers from the burning. She loves the Catholic priest Ralph de Bricassart to madness and distraction, and the story of their anguish is the main thread running through this opulent, *Gone With The Wind* saga. But this forbidden love is another goad driving her on to marry Luke, as she plainly sees:

> *Well, that was that. She had committed herself, there could be no turning back. In a few weeks, or however long it took to call banns, she would marry Luke O'Neill. She would be . . . Mrs Luke O'Neill! How strange! Why did she say yes? Because HE told me I must, HE said I was to do it. But why? To remove HIM from danger? To protect himself, or me? Ralph de Bricassart, sometimes I think I hate you . . .*

Marry or burn, says the old proverb. It's Meggie's tragedy that she has to do both. Her marriage is ill-starred from the first, and she soon becomes yet another of the female victims sacrificed on the altar of matrimony.

For all these sufferers, women and men too, the experience of harsh reality is made even more bitter by the hopes and dreams that they have to put away. They have to live with their sadness in the knowledge that it does not have to be thus — that others have found in marriage not a trap, but a lifelong comfort and joy.

Farewell, Beloved

Of all sad words of tongue and pen,
The saddest are, 'It might have been'.

John Greenleaf Whittier

AMONG THE ANNALS OF MARRIAGE PROPOSALS, a special chapel of remembrance hung with rosemary and rue must be set aside for those which however deeply desired, are not fated to succeed. Many couples do not manage to make the step from private love to public commitment. They do not get the marriage act together, for any number of reasons.

A touching compromise is that arranged by Hemingway's legendary lovers in *A Farewell To Arms*. He, a wounded soldier, and she his nurse are carrying on a clandestine love affair which would result in her dismissal and their separation if it came to light:

> It was lovely in the nights, and if we could only touch each other we were happy. Besides all the big times we had many small ways of making love . . .
>
> We said to each other that we were married the first day that she had come to the hospital, and we counted months from our wedding day. I wanted to be really married, but Catherine said if we were they would send her away . . .

'Maybe they wouldn't.'

'They would. They'd send me home and then we'd be apart till after the war.'

'I'd come on leave.'

'You couldn't get to Scotland and back on leave. Besides, I won't leave you. What good would it do to marry now? We're really married. We couldn't be any more married.'

'I only want to for you.'

'There isn't any me. I'm you. Don't make up a separate me . . .'

'All right. But I'll marry you the day you say.'

Tragically, the day never comes. Casualties alike of the war and of their love, the couple escape the hostilities only to face personal catastrophe. Catherine becomes pregnant and after a horrifying labour loses both her baby and her life. The novel ends as the desolate lover walks off alone into the rain, sole survivor of a doomed, unmarried love.

More commonly the near misses of aspiring suitors are pathetic rather than tragic. Some even raise failure to the level of comedy. Judge Samuel Sewall was a key figure in the early days of the US, when he served as one of the judges at the Salem witchcraft trials in 1692. His first wife bore him 14 children and then expired; his second wife died in May 1720. At the age of 68 Judge Sewall immediately embarked upon one of the most celebrated courtships in American history, his wooing of Madam Katherine Winthrop.

Clearly the judge got off on the wrong foot by telling Madam Winthrop, as he recorded in his diary, 'my loving wife having died so soon and so suddenly, 'twas hardly convenient for me to think of marrying again'. When he then proposed marriage to her a mere *two days* later, she understandably turned him down flat.

But pioneer men were made of stern stuff. Undeterred, Sewall gave her a week to think it over, and left her a book of devotional verse to improve her mind (and his chances?) But only four days later he was back again, where he found that 'Madam seemed to harp upon the same string' as before, and refused him again – as well she might, having herself survived twelve 'birthings', been widowed twice, and at 56 years of age looking forward to a quieter life!

Next Sewall decided to appeal to Madam's body rather than her mind, and gave her a piece of cake and some gingerbread. But he could not resist sending her subsequently a copy of 'Mr Mayhew's sermon, and Account of the State of the Indians on Martha's Vineyard'. When he called on her the following day, Madam Winthrop had obviously decided that she had been too courteous with her persistent admirer. The time had come to give him the elbow. As the judge told his diary:

> *Madam Winthrop's countenance was much changed from what 'twas on Monday, looked dark and glowering . . . had some converse, but very cold and indifferent.*

Despite yet another rejection, Sewall continued to treat himself as the impending husband. He tried to make business arrangements with her, installed himself in her house to read another religious tract hysterically entitled 'Dr Sibb's Bowels Opened: Or, A Discovery Of The Union Betwixt Christ And The Church', and demanded to know 'when our proceedings should be made public'.

It is impossible to tally with any certainty the number of proposals made by this tenacious oldster as he kept pressing his unwelcome suit with yet more books of sermons and bags of sugared almonds. The turning-point came when Madam Winthrop told him bluntly that she had lost interest in the sexual side of marriage. At this he lost interest in her! But within a few months he had married one Mary Gibbs Shrimpton, presumably a woman of a more obliging disposition. His proposal to her is not recorded.

As this shows, a woman can sometimes have an *embarras de* proposals. It takes both luck and good juggling to get the right man in the right order. Thackeray's 'brilliant little woman' Becky Sharp makes it the business of her life to catch a rich husband, preferably titled too, in the high society of *Vanity Fair*. As a governess in the house of Sir Pitt Crawley, Becky makes a conquest of the hideous old coot by her looks, style and deft management of affairs. Then she moves to another post. But when his ailing wife providentially dies, Sir Pitt wastes no time in trying to win back this treasure:

> *'I want to see you, Miss Becky,' said Sir Pitt. 'Come along a me into the parlour,' and they entered that apartment together.*
>
> *'I wawnt you back at Queen's Crawley, Miss,' the Baronet said, fixing his eyes upon her, and taking off his hat with its great crepe mourning band. His eyes had such a strange look, and fixed on her so steadfastly, that Rebecca Sharp began almost to tremble . . .*
>
> *'I tell you I WANT you. I'm going back to the Vuneral. Will you come back? Yes or no?'*

Sharp by name and sharp by nature, Becky is not as a rule slow on the uptake. But in the agitation of the moment she is not clear about what is going on. The Baronet becomes more explicit, if not more elegant:

> *'You must come back. Do come back. Dear Becky, do come.'*
> *'Come — as what, sir?' Rebecca gasped out.*

'Come as Lady Crawley if you like,' the Baronet said, grasping his crepe hat. 'There! Will that zatisfy you? Come back and be my wife. You're vit vor't. Birth be hanged. You're as good a lady as ever I see. You've got more brains in your little vinger than any baronet's wife in the country. Will you come? Yes or no?'

'O Sir Pitt!' Rebecca said, very much moved.

'Say yes, Becky,' Sir Pitt continued. 'I'm an old man, but a good 'n. I'll make you happy, zee if I don't. You shall do what you like; spend what you like; and av it all your own way. I'll make you a zettlement. I'll do everything reglar. Look year!' and the old man fell down on his knees and leered at her like a satyr.

Perfect! Everything that Becky has schemed for — a rich, landed, titled gent, besotted and antiquated in equal proportions. But it is not to be. Becky weeps 'some of the most genuine tears that ever fell from her eyes'. For never dreaming of such a stroke of luck, Becky has tried to scramble into the baronetcy from one rung lower down. She is already married — to Sir Pitt's son!

Becky is fated never to become Lady Crawley. But sometimes the loser lives to fight another day. More poignant still are those proposals which hover on the brink of fulfilment rather than living on into reality.

No one conveys the sensation of love holding its breath better than Dick Francis, a master of the experience of unfulfilled longing. His heroes, bruised and bemused by life's rough passage, can see new love glimmering and growing but hardly dare to hope that it can be for them. The defeats of the past have taught them that loving means losing, and the loser left with nothing but a legacy of painful memories and stifled sighs.

Sighs and the three-dot ending are very much the mood

of Francis' marvellous novel, *Knock Down*. The hero falls hopelessly for a girl whose cool exterior conceals the pain of a damaged heart imperfectly restored after the death of her lover. She is drawn to him, too, but can they risk being hurt again?

Sophie telephoned at nine o'clock that evening. Her voice sounded so immediately familiar that it was incredible to think that I had known her for less than twenty-four hours . . .

She said, 'How are your knight in shining armour instincts?'

'Rusty.'

'I could provide Brasso.'

I smiled. 'What do you want done?'

'Yes. Mm. When it comes to the point, I don't know that I've got any right to ask.'

'Will you marry me?' I said.

'WHAT did you say?'

'Er . . .' I said. 'Never mind. What was it you wanted done?'

'Yes,' she said.

'Yes what?'

'Yes, I will. Marry you.'

I stared across the office, seeing nothing. I hadn't meant to ask her. Or had I? Anyway, not so soon. I swallowed. Cleared my throat.

'Then . . . you've a right to ask anything.'

'Good,' she said crisply. 'Button your ears back . . .'

'Right,' I wrote it down. 'Are you working tomorrow evening?'

'No. Saturday morning.'

'Then . . . I could come to your place . . . on my way home . . .'

'Yes.' *Her voice was tentative, almost embarrassed.* 'I
live . . .'

'I know where you live,' *I said.* 'Somewhere at the end
of the five-furlong straight of Sandown racecourse . . . I'll
be there.'

'I've got to go now, or I'll be late.' *She paused, then said
doubtfully,* 'Did you mean it?'

'Yes,' *I said.* 'I think so. Did you?'

'No,' *she said.* 'It's silly.'

In these encounters the moment when the proposal of
marriage is offered, and not accepted, forms the emotional
climax of the affair. After this all the rest is a sad decline,
full of reminders of how it used to be, as in this
unforgettable exchange between the two doomed lovers in
the 1937 movie, *Camille*. Garbo gives her finest performance as the ill-fated Camille, flashing from magical
radiance to elegant restraint with her lover, Armand.

She is a wealthy cocotte, while he comes from a
respectable family. In nineteenth-century Paris they are
worlds apart. But their love is strong enough to bridge
the chasm between them, and they come together for
one idyllic summer at a country cottage. There they
attend a wedding, which gives rise to the trembling
hope that their own love for each other is strong enough
to build on:

GARBO: *Don't ever leave me!*
ARMAND: *I never will — but you — I can't bear our
          summer to end —*
GARBO: *Nor I.*
ARMAND: *Could you go on living like this?*
GARBO: *I couldn't live any other way now . . .*
ARMAND: *You mean you'd give up everything for me?*
GARBO: *Everything in the world, everything.*

THEY KISS

GARBO: *Never be jealous again. Never doubt that I love you more than the world, more than myself.*

ARMAND: *Then — marry me.*

GARBO: *What?*

ARMAND: *I married you today. Every word the priest said was meant for us. In my heart I made all the vows to you.*

GARBO: *And I to you.*

ARMAND: *Then —*

GARBO: *No, no — that isn't fitting. Let me love you, let me live for you — don't let me ask any more from Heaven than that — God might get angry.*

Garbo's last speech here has the same emotional power as the last line of another famous weepie of the black, white and silver screen, *Now Voyager* (1942): 'Don't let's ask for the moon, when we have had the stars.'

America is another country. It's constantly surprising that the new world can be so full of old pain. Surely the unmatched and unmatchable master of the moment of loss is F. Scott Fitzgerald. The situation of two people who are desperately in love yet who cannot overcome all the obstacles that keep them apart was one that haunted him all his life. It comes up in his very first story, and appears finally in the novel that he was writing at the time of his death, *The Last Tycoon*. This was a legacy of his own love and marriage with the beautiful Southern belle Zelda Sayre, which began and ended in such unhappiness that it obliterated all the good years in between.

Fitzgerald first created this situation in *This Side Of Paradise*, a book to fall in love by, if ever there was one. As Rosalind and Amory fall in love . . .

> *. . . they were together constantly, for lunch, for dinner, and nearly every evening — always in a sort of breathless hush, as if they feared that any minute the spell would break and drop them out of this paradise of rose and flame. But the spell became a trance, seemed to increase from day to day; they began to talk of marrying in July — in June. All life was transmitted into terms of their love, all experience, all desires, all ambitions were nullified: 'She's life and hope and happiness, my whole world now.'*

But they have no money to marry on, and in the ensuing tension, they break apart. Despite her cry 'Lover! Lover! I can't do with you, and I can't imagine life without you', Rosalind ends it — she can't bear to drift down from the heights where they have been so passionately happy. Yet even as she sends him away, she knows that she has lost something for ever, something irreplaceable.

Fitzgerald returned to this theme even more powerfully in his masterpiece, *The Great Gatsby*. Gatsby and Daisy fall deeply, lyrically in love, and pledge themselves to each other in physical and emotional passion. But then he is sent overseas as a soldier, and Daisy cannot withstand the pressures of life on her own:

> *All night the saxophone wailed the hopeless comment of the 'Beale Street Blues' while a hundred pairs of gold and silver slippers shuffled in the shining dust. At the grey tea hour there were always rooms that throbbed incessantly with this low, sweet fever, while fresh faces drifted here and there like rose petals blown by the sad horns around the floor.*

So Daisy begins to dance to 'the sadness and suggestiveness of life in new tunes'. Gatsby, like so many American heroes, is a man out of nowhere. He has no money and no position. Daisy is locked into her world of riches, assurance and privilege like a maiden in a castle to which Gatsby cannot find the key. His bid to hold her fails, and he never recovers from this loss:

> . . . *he found himself committed to the following of a grail . . . She vanished into her rich house, into her rich, full life, leaving Gatsby — nothing. He felt married to her, that was all . . . He stretched out his hand desperately as if to snatch a wisp of air, to save a fragment of the spot that she had made lovely for him. But it was all going by too fast now for his blurred eyes and he knew that he had lost that part of it, the freshest and the best, for ever.*

Haunted by the belief that 'rich girls don't marry poor boys, Jay Gatsby', as Daisy mockingly whispers in his imagination, Gatsby devotes the rest of his life to becoming what Daisy might want. Only death can free him from this quest.

As the Hemingway story showed, death is the last great enemy of love's promise, and it is one that even the strongest cannot defeat. Ian Fleming's James Bond finds as 007 that he is always closer to danger and destruction than other men. But when, *On Her Majesty's Secret Service*, he encounters the beautiful Teresa, he has other things on his mind:

> *Bond suddenly thought, Hell! I'll never find another girl like this one. She's got everything I've looked for in a woman. She's beautiful, in bed and out. She's adventurous, brave, resourceful. She's exciting always. She seems to love me. She'd let me go on with my life. She's a lone girl, not cluttered up with friends, relations, belongings. Above all, she needs me. It'll be someone for me to look after. I'm fed up with all these untidy, casual affairs that leave me with*

*a bad conscience. I wouldn't mind having children. I've got
no social background into which she would or wouldn't fit.
We're two of a pair, really. Why not make it for always?*

*Bond found his voice saying those words that he had
never said in his life before, never expected to say.*

'Tracy. I love you. Will you marry me?'

The whirlwind romance is followed by an equally whirlwind
marriage. At last the two lovers can be alone together;
'we've got all the time in the world', says Bond contentedly.
But as they drive away to start their honeymoon, a bullet
from an unseen enemy destroys his hopes for ever:

*Bond turned towards Tracy. She was lying forward with
her face buried in the ruins of the steering wheel. Her pink
handkerchief had come off and the bell of golden hair hung
down and hid her face. Bond put his arm round her
shoulders, across which the dark patches had begun to
flower.*

*He pressed her against him. He looked up at the young
patrolman and smiled his reassurance.*

*'It's all right,' he said in a clear voice as if explaining
something to a child. 'It's quite all right. She's having a
rest. We'll be going on soon. There's no hurry. You see —'
Bond's head sank down against hers and he whispered into
her hair — 'you see, we've got all the time in the world.'*

Anyone who has ever lost someone they love knows that it
takes all the time in the world to come to terms with it.
For Time is a slow doctor, and he works without anaesthetic, as Stevie Smith says in her *Novel On Yellow Paper*:

*And this causes a great deal of sadness and wildness and
despair. And you turn this way and that way, and there
is nothing, there is nothing to be done at all, for all the
wildness and tears and despair. You have lost. Suddenly*

*you have lost everything, and the hours are long, and only
a thousand hours will help at all to heal.*

Well, you have the time. When you have lost everything
else, it's all you do have. The reality of high risks taken
and dangers averted by successful lovers is nowhere more
clearly demonstrated than in the sadness and desolation of
those who lose.

II

Immodest Proposals

*'Let's make a little gentle pornography
with one another.'*

The Art Of The Proposition

Now boys, three cheers for Venus, hip hip hip hooray.
Oh how I enjoy sex and oh how I enjoy it. There have
been many funny things about sex in my life that have
made me laugh and so now I will tell you

Stevie Smith

'WILL YOU BE MINE?' This question which enshrines the classic marriage proposal can and does carry another meaning. Not all love encounters are fated to end in marriage. Ardent suitors frequently have something more immediate in view.

As every woman knows, for every proposal of marriage you get at least twenty propositions. Even with the best willy in the world a man can only marry one woman at a time, and that isn't usually sufficient to exhaust his interest in the opposite sex. So after a decent interval (and sometimes not even that!) married men rejoin their single brothers in the chase. And central to their concerns once more becomes the compelling thought of jollies, and how to get them.

This isn't how it's supposed to be, of course. The love story always used to rise to its triumphant climax at the altar, after which, we were told, 'they lived happily ever after'. And so they may, and millions do. But not necessarily with each other, or only with each other. Some men (and women) can't manage without a ménage, and three seems an unduly self-denying number of partners in these liberated days.

But partners, whether sexual or matrimonial, still have to be wooed and won. 'The act of love lies somewhere between the belly and the mind', according to Roger McGough. And somewhere between complete indifference and full commitment lies the proposition.

A proposition is generally taken to be a very different transaction from a proposal. But it is closely related to its more respectable brother, if on the wrong side of the blanket. The one may be only the other in undress, so to speak. A nationwide survey of couples about to be married in 1983 discovered that while most proposals are still made over a romantic dinner for two, or on bended knee, 'a notable number are now made in bed'. So it's true that one thing really does lead to another!

Of the twin transactions, the proposition is the one that has shown a far more vigorous rate of activity than the proposal. Men think very seriously before popping the question, and will only propose two or three times at most in their entire lives. But they'll proposition much more freely, on the 'you can't win the raffle if you don't buy a ticket' principle. One highly successful propositioner explained his secret, which like all schemes of sheer genius was based on the utmost simplicity:

It's like this. I just ask all the women I meet. Then if only half of them say yes, I'm getting 50% more than I would have anyway.

As you see, the beauty of this system is its utter transparency. Percentages or no, you don't have to be a leading mathematician to apply it — just a perennial optimist with the hide of a rhino.

The amount of propositioning that goes on is quite amazing, but for the most part these heroic endeavours are unacknowledged and unsung. They simply don't come up as a subject of what my beloved mother used to call Polite Conversation. Yet it's going on, in life and literature, enthusiastically, all the time. Blush not, gentle reader! 'Let other pens dwell on guilt and misery', invited Jane Austen when she hove in sight of the illicit jollies at the end of *Mansfield Park*. And they have, dear reader, they have!

For not all hopeful admirers are men of honour. One woman's prince is another one's toad, and the knight *inside* his shining armour is just an old wicked seducer, the eternal opportunist bent on getting something for nothing but the price of asking. While some men have vexed their souls worrying about how to deliver a proposal, others have exercised their wits on how to phrase a proposition — the other side of the same coin that buys a woman's consent.

How to ask for IT? and successfully? Much mental effort has gone into the demands of this game. It is in fact the leading leisure activity of the entire population apart from infants and the hopelessly insane. It has only remained uncommercialized because no one's going to pay for what they can find all about them, in highways and byeways, country lanes or city streets. And a modest but regular level of fun is expected by every red-blooded member of the human race — you don't have to be a US citizen to feel that you are entitled to life, liberty, and the happiness of pursuit.

Girls spend years building up the know-how necessary to handle this monstrous regiment of men on the make. Luckily most of them turn out to be squaddies from the Brigade of Gunners — they're gonna do this and they're gonna do that, but they're all flash and no bang because there's not enough lead in their pellets to make the stub of a blunt pencil. But that still leaves enough men who are licensed to injure if not kill a lady, and a girl's education in self-defence against these 003½s starts at an early age. There used to be a skipping game at my school of Mixed Infants which built up to the triumphant rhythmic climax of little females chanting in unison:

> *I WOULD if I COULD*
> *But I WANT to be GOOD*
> *And I'm NOT that KIND of a GIRL!*

Girls need to perfect their no-how, because men have so many different methods of trying to get them to say yes:

> *There are nine and sixty ways*
> *Of constructing tribal lays —*
> *And every single one of them is right!*

wrote Rudyard Kipling. This number must indicate the total of possible variant passes *per man*, not per tribe, race or nation. Women are reminded that nine and sixty represents an option, not an obligation — if you don't like it, leave it alone. And they can't all be right — or not all the time. A chap has to expect to get it wrong now and then . . .

> *She started to cry on his shoulder and he held her very tight. He took a long chance.*
> *'Sleep with me.'*
> *'No, baby,' she said sympathetically.*
> *'Please, please . . . just once.'*
> *'I can't, honey. I don't love you.'*

Who said anything about love? Our hero, from Nathanael West's scorching portrayal of low-life Hollywood, *The Day*

Of The Locust, is not after any such high flight. Not satisfied with this bungled pass, he tries another throw. This time he hits right below the belt, in reminding the unfortunate object of his attentions that she has worked as a call-girl:

> 'You worked for Mrs Jennings. Make believe you're still working for her.'
>   She didn't get angry.
>   'That was a mistake. And anyway that was different. I only went on call enough times to pay for the funeral, and besides those men were complete strangers. You know what I mean?'
>   'Yes. But please, darling. I'll never bother you again. I'll go East right after. Be kind.'
>   'I can't.'
>   'Why . . .?'
>   'I just can't. I'm sorry, darling. I'm not a tease, but I can't like that.'
>   'I love you.'
>   'No, sweetheart, I can't.'

See what some girls have to put up with? First the insult, then the phoney sweet-talk and emotional blackmail, and finally the thundering lie, 'I love you'. Somehow it's not quite enough when he breaks his ankle at the end of the story. Poetic justice requires that the injury really ought to be sustained to his middle leg.

As this shows, making a good proposition is no easier than making a good proposal. When propositioning most men are blissfully unaware of what a funny figure they cut, with one foot in their mouths and the other on the banana skin. Being a king-sized lady-puller doesn't seem to do a lot for a man's technique. Did anyone ever tell Richard Burton, for instance, seen here through the eyes of Joan Collins . . .?

'Did anyone ever tell you you look pretty with short hair?' he said, casually moving his hand down lower.

'Yes,' I said, firmly removing the roving hand, and squinting up at the gorgeous greenish eyes, now a foot from mine . . .

'Why don't you relax,' he whispered, his hand fiddling with the ties on my bikini top. 'None of the crew can see us.'

'I am relaxed,' I said gaily, 'relaxed and lying in the sun and thinking about my boy-friend ARTHUR!'

He looked at me and we both smiled.

'I'll get you yet, Miss Collins,' he said lightly, and then proceeded to tell me vivid details about his seductions and conquests of the actresses he had worked with — on stage and screen!

However did he get a reputation for charm?

Less crude but still corny was Clark Gable's approach to Carole Lombard on their first date. He asked her back to his flat for coffee after dinner. Gifted with a wicked sense of humour, Lombard took her cue to say, 'Who the hell do you think you are, Clark Gable?' The discomfited King of Hollywood sat there fuming, and couldn't think of a thing to say. But then, as Ava Gardner once said, he was the kind of man that if you said 'Hello, Clark, how are you?' he'd be kinda stuck for an answer.

Not all men are wolves in gorilla's clothing. There is a successful proposition for every unsuccessful one, and many men discover for themselves the truth of the old biblical adage, 'ask, and it shall be given you; seek, and ye shall find'. They don't have to be great stylists. They simply have to make a woman feel as if they mean it for her, and for her alone. If they can do that, they can get away with the most . . . laid-back approaches.

Some men actually specialize in offering themselves with an off-hand shrug, simply as an interlude in the long boredom of life. Gallic lovers are expert in the invitation to keep *ennui* at bay, as a game for two players. Françoise Sagan's Luc is the type of man to drive any woman wild with desire — sexy, inscrutable, irresistible. He doesn't even bother to court the heroine of Sagan's first famous teenage-confessional novel. He just tells her what's on the agenda:

> *I want to possess you, to spend a night with you.*
>
> *I never thought . . . I never thought I would come to admire you. I do very much, Dominique. I love you very much. I can't promise to love you for 'ever and ever' as children say, but we are very alike, you know.*
>
> *I not only want to sleep with you, I want to lie with you, go away with you on holiday. We would be very happy, very loving. I would show you the sea, teach you about money, and how to feel more free. We'd be less bored, that's all.*

It may be all, but it's enough. In fact, it's fantastic. I nearly fell for a man purely because he asked me to go with him to the Arpège. The Arpège? I found out afterwards he meant the Ardèche, but what the hell. In this case, he wasn't quite enough. But Luc is more than enough for Dominique. She accepts his offer, and with her eyes wide open says *'Bonjour, Tristesse'* like thousands of women before and since.

But surely the uncrowned king of the proposition was the writer, artist and sex athlete Frank Harris. If he succeeded with women even half the times he claimed he had, he ought to be in the *Guinness Book of Records*. Harris had two shots in his locker that most would-be sex maniacs haven't got. First of all, he *liked* women, while many men who dog females ferociously seem to be moved more by hatred and contempt than by love. And then again, he had the wit to vary his approaches, instead of coming up with the same tired old fish pâté every time.

Harris had a tremendous repertoire of compliments and blandishments, and never used the same line twice. His simplest was:

Won't you come to me tonight?

and that, after an ardent courtship, melted the knickers off the lovely Irene in Athens. For a colder clime, he would try:

Imagine we're on a desert island together – alone!

With a sterner race of women like the Nordic or Anglo-Saxon species, he had a more spiritual approach, quoting Browning, and singing love songs in Italian (his *basso profundo* was much admired). And in case they got the idea that he was only after their bodies, he would offer to show them 'all the kingdoms of the spirit'. You've got to admit that the guy had style.

Some people (especially jealous male people) have taken leave to doubt Harris's racy amorous autobiography. But supportive evidence exists from one of his lovers, the distinguished writer Enid Bagnold. In her long and full life, the memory of a Harris proposition lived for her in all its freshness. 'Sex is the gateway to life!' he told her thrillingly. And she records:

So I went through the gateway to life
in an upper room at the Café Royal.

Now that's the art of the proposition – poetry in motion! If only it could always be like that!

Have Some Madeira, M'Dear

> *Oh maiden, let your distaff be,*
> *And pace the flowery meads with me,*
> *And I will tell you lies . . .*
>
> *Oh follow me where love is flown,*
> *Into the leafy woods alone,*
> *And I will work you ill.*

A. E. Housman

ONCE UPON A TIME, long ago and far away, men didn't just up and out with it. They expected to have to court the chosen lady, to flatter, to persuade, to beat down a real resistance. They had to stoke up the fires of passion if they hoped to build up a head of steam. Every man knew that no self-respecting woman would drop her drawers for him on sight, no matter how badly he was giving her ants in the pants. In those days a man had to learn how to woo and to wait if he wanted to work his wicked way with you — in other words, to seduce.

Seduction is a dying art, like everything else that was invented before telephones, trains and planes. In today's world, the pace of modern life doesn't permit it. If there's only six hours between flights, that's all the time you've got to have lift-off with the dreamy guy you've been pretending not to look at all the way from New York. Sure, he could be a champion miler or even a marathon man, given time and encouragement and a following wind. But the time factor makes it a sprint, baby, and you don't want to be jumping up and down on the starting-line while he's deciding, 'This is not my distance'.

The art of the seduction is closely allied to the art of the proposal. The secret is to make a woman want to so much, that nothing in the world would stop her from saying yes. In these circumstances the true artist shines to his full advantage. A friend of mine confessed how the care and flair of a man she'd never really noticed before really won her over.

He had asked her to go for a day by the sea, and had obviously taken pains with the arrangements. He'd hired an open-top sports car, fixed a big hamper, and all that. But it wasn't the smart car, the super picnic, the dinner afterwards with soft lights and sweet music that seduced her. It was the fact that when he called for her in the car, on the passenger seat lay a chiffon scarf that he had bought specially so that the wind wouldn't ruin her hair. This one touch of thoughtfulness went straight to her heart and made her his, and when she melted into his arms later that night, she was still wearing the chiffon, if nothing else.

As with all artists, it's a pleasure to watch them work. The first step for the seducer is to arouse a woman's interest, usually by presenting himself as a sensitive plant that the world has bruised in some mysterious way. This can be used by women too, and it works like a charm for the heroine of *The French Lieutenant's Woman*. It is used again by Rodolphe in his seduction of Flaubert's *Madame Bovary*.

Rodolphe has been deeply struck by the heroine's pale face and dark eyes at first sight. But she is sexually unawakened, despite the fact that she is married to a boorish country doctor. How to rouse a Sleeping Beauty? Rodolphe begins with a passionate declaration that some souls are destined by fate to love. He makes a profound impact upon Emma Bovary:

> *She saw little gleams of gold playing about his dark pupils. She was near enough to him to smell the cream on his glossy hair. She felt limp . . .*

The average Englishwoman, reared on nothing more erotic in the way of masculine perfume than Imperial Leather and Coal Tar soap, could go limp just reading this. But Rodolphe does not rely on copious sloshes of the old Eau Sauvage alone. He proves to have a superb turn of phrase, plus a terrific romantic dash and assurance. 'You cannot fight with fate!' he declares, 'or resist when the angels smile.'

Finally he comes to take her out riding. He has made himself look stunning in a velvet riding jacket, white breeches, and his finest leather boots. But best of all, the horse he has brought for Emma has been prepared as for a princess, with a side-saddle of softest buckskin, and pink rosettes tucked behind its ears!

Together they ride deep into the heart of the woodland, in 'a medley of grey and fawn and gold'. Here Rodolphe declares his love with the thrilling question:

> *Are not our destinies now one?*

Like a shy creature of the forest, Emma is startled and on the point of flight. But Rodolphe is gentle and reassuring. Tenderly he builds to a wonderful emotional climax no woman could resist:

> *'You are in my heart as a Madonna on a pedestal, lifted high, secure and immaculate . . . Only, I can't live*

without you. I need you, your eyes, your voice, your thoughts! Oh, be my friend, my sister, my angel!' . . .

Silence was everywhere. Sweetness seemed to breathe from the trees. She felt her heart beginning to beat again, and the blood flowing inside her flesh like a river of milk . . . Now was her hour of triumph. Love, so long pent up within her, surged forth at last with a wild and joyous flow, and she savoured it without remorse, disquiet or distress.

Isn't that glorious? To fall into the arms of love, and in the very heart of nature, too. There's something uniquely wonderful about a passionate *affaire du coeur*, all for love and the world well lost. It's an experience every woman owes herself. Even if it ends in tears, you have known what it is to scale the heights, a secret known only to a few. And you can always say to yourself those brilliant, rueful, forgiving words of Browning:

> *How sad and bad and mad it was –*
> *But then, how it was sweet!*

Rodolphe is of course the ideal seducer, handsome, rich, sexy and *unmarried*. But unhandsome, unsexy, unrich and unsingle men need not despair. It ain't what you are, it's the way that you are it, as Theodore Dreiser shows in his epic novel, *Jennie Gerhardt*.

Jennie is both lovely and vulnerable, which attracts the attention of more than one admirer. But her men, though not Rodolphes, are not the heartless villains of the stereotype seducer, Victorian-style. They are warm, they are loving, and they care about her. Dreiser puts in a plea for the surrender to this love, that must strike a whole hallelujah chorus of chords for men and women alike:

From all enchanted things of earth and air, this preciousness has been drawn . . . A hundred years of cowslips, bluebells, violets; purple spring and golden autumn; sunshine, shower and dewy mornings; the night immortal; all the rhythm of time unrolling. A chronicle unwritten and past all power of writing; who shall preserve a record of the petals that fell from the roses a century ago? . . .

If you have understood and appreciated the beauty of harebells three hundred times repeated; if the quality of the roses, of the music, of the ruddy mornings and evenings of the world has ever touched your heart; if all beauty were passing, and you were given these things to hold in your arms before the world slipped away —

would you give them up?

Lovers have in general shown a remarkable capacity for not giving up. The test of a true lover after all is his persistence in hanging on, not dropping off. And many a man has triumphantly converted a skin of the teeth situation into a palpable hit.

A lover who is more than ready for the strike is Andrew Marvell. One of the most famous propositions of all time is the poetical reproach he addressed *To His Coy Mistress* some time in the swinging seventeenth century. The time and effort he's invested in the seduction has led him to feel he's overdue for his reward. Why doesn't she come through?

This witty poem has had a comical history. It always appears in anthologies under 'Love Poems', whereas in reality it's a sparkling piece of aggro, obviously written in a fit of teeth-grinding frustration.

> *Had we but world enough, and time,*
> *This coyness, lady, were no crime*

he begins, nastily. It's just like the way men start to call you 'Darling' when they're getting ratty. And Marvell's lady has really been getting up his nose. We haven't got for ever for this, he goes on:

> *For at my back I always hear*
> *Time's winged chariot hurrying near.*

What he means is that he's not prepared to chase her any more. He has been fobbed off for what he considers far too long (about two weeks?) And from the lady's point of view, 'no' was the only safe contraceptive in the days when rigid self-control and brilliant timing, or unappetizing devices of kidskin and sponge, must have made sex more of an ordeal than a pleasure!

But the poet has come to the end of his rope and found it frayed. Enough of the seduction — what about the real stuff? This is in fact no love poem but an ultimatum. 'Come through or else' is the message.

It's not exactly new and original. The 'we're running out of time' ploy has a long and ancient history. It goes all the way back to the Greeks and it's still in service. One of my girl-friends owes her existence to the historic moment when President Kennedy called Kruschev's bluff over the Bay of Pigs. 'The world trembles on the brink of disaster,' her father told her mother. 'A nuclear holocaust is brewing. Or worse. Come to bed tonight, in case we aren't here tomorrow.' Well, she did, and what do you know it still was, and what's more, another little earthling was due for touchdown approximately nine months later.

Andrew Marvell has another lever, too. You will get old and ugly, he says, and no one will want you then. And what's the point of hanging on to your virginity, if you're only saving it for the worms:

> *For yonder all before us lie*
> *Deserts of vast eternity.*

♡ 124 ♡

> *Thy beauty shall no more be found,*
> *Nor in the marble vault shall sound*
> *My echoing song: then worms shall try*
> *That long-preserved virginity.*
> *The grave's a fine and private place,*
> *But none, I think, do there embrace.*

This final touch of the Edgar Allan Poes is surely enough to make every fibre of female flesh creep on your bones. But would it make you risk your little all, and leap into his second-best bed? It's funny how often men can come out with something that is guaranteed to produce the opposite effect from the happy outcome (or in-come) that they are seeking.

Chief among those who want to have it both ways, and are determined *anyway* to have it *some* way is D. H. Lawrence. His emotional autobiography in *Sons and Lovers* is a revelation of his powers of persistence. Nevertheless he's a skilless and self-absorbed seducer. He just keeps beavering away towards what he knows is out there somewhere, the consummation devoutly to be wished. Miriam is the long-term girlfriend and soulmate of the DHL character, Paul, and the luckless recipient of this heavy-handed pass:

> *In the darkness, where he could not see her but only feel her, his passion flooded him. He clasped her very close.*
>
> *'Some time you will have me?' he murmured, hiding his face on her shoulder. It was so difficult.*
>
> *'Not now,' she said.*
>
> *His hopes and his heart sank. A dreariness came over him.*
>
> *'No,' he said.*
>
> *His clasp of her slackened . . .*

But Lawrence has not earned his title as the champion of what he dubbed 'The Primary Relation' for nothing. After an interlude of argy-bargy, Paul returns to the hanky-panky:

> *'We belong to each other,' he said.*
> *'Yes.'*
> *'Then why shouldn't we belong to each other altogether?'*
> *'But —' she faltered.*
> *'I know it's a lot to ask,' he said; 'but there's not much risk for you really — not in the Gretchen way. You can trust me there?'*

The Gretchen way? Is this one the pillow-books haven't taught us? At this moment, any romance flies out of the window. The lumpen introduction of the obscure but unmistakable reference to primitive contraceptive techniques gives the game away — love laughs at blocksmiths.

Maybe we shouldn't be too hard on Paul for this limp and gauche seduction attempt. He had inherited what was, by this time, a dying form. The great hey-day of the seduction was the nineteenth century, when men were men and women didn't know the difference.

The seduction proper, the real thing, was on its way out as soon as girls began to learn which way the grass grew. But it had had its hour. And it did ensure for male-female relations a certain finesse that would still be welcome today!

Please Please Me

> '*You do love me?*'
> '*I really love you. I'm crazy about you.*
> *Come on, please.*'
> '*You really love me?*'
> '*Don't keep saying that. Come on. Please, please,*
> *Catherine.*'
> '*You can't. You shouldn't —*'
> '*Come on. Don't talk. Please come on.*'

Ernest Hemingway, A Farewell To Arms

THE SEDUCTION may be a thing of the past. But the thing itself lingers on. The present is usually bursting with one damn thing after another, whichever way a woman turns. Or rather, with the same damn thing over and over, as Edna Ferber once said. So if a girl's going to be propositioned up hill and down dale, she should expect it to be a thing of beauty, if not a joy for ever.

Every woman should stick to this requirement as her bottom line, so to speak, no matter how unpromising the material she's working with. I saw a girl at a fabulous summer ball in an ancient Oxford college, half-sitting, half-lying on a flight of worm-eaten and none too clean oak stairs. Her escort, one of those titled chimpanzees in which the university abounds, was fighting his way through the froth and frou-frou of her ball-gown to crawl all over her. She retained her perfect finishing-school composure in this compromising public situation, but her well-bred tones were repeatedly to be heard insisting:

You might ask me nicely. You might say please.

Asking nicely isn't just a matter of saying please, naturally. Reduce it all to ps and qs and what you finish up with is wham-bam-thankyou-ma'am. It's more to do with an approach that is subtle, graceful, stylish. One where the base intentions are not sticking out like a well-known pair of royal ears. One which believes that if a girl's worth doing, she's worth doing well.

It helps a lot if the chap has a poetical turn in him. All women have a secret longing to be wooed in verse. You can adore any man who quotes poetry to you – just as long as he isn't pretending to be the author of the tender phrases of Shakespeare and Keats that he's murmuring into your receptive shell-like. So here are some handy poetical propositions for the man who wants to take his act up-market. My favourite is a sprightly little 'to the woods' ballad from the sixteenth century by Christopher Marlowe:

> *Come live with me and be my love,*
> *And we will all the pleasures prove*
> *That valleys, groves and hills and fields,*
> *Woods or steepy mountains yields.*
>
> *And I will make thee beds of roses*
> *And a thousand fragrant posies,*
> *A cap of flowers, and a kirtle*
> *Embroidered all with leaves of myrtle.*
>
> *A belt of straw and ivy buds,*
> *With coral clasps and amber studs,*

And if these pleasures thee may move,
Come live with me and be my love.

The shepherd swains shall dance and sing
For thy delight each May morning.
If such delights thy mind may move
Come live with me and be my love.

Now there you are — fresh as a daisy and coming up roses is the question every woman is waiting to be asked. Especially on a hot summer day. One hopeful urban pastoralist discovered for himself the value of this approach. Coming home from work on the 143 bus to Islington he sat opposite a flower-like girl in white, who was obviously wilting under the combined effects of a long London day and a steaming midsummer. He caught her eye and whispered:

I know a bank where the wild thyme blows.

He had to stop there as he couldn't remember the next bit, even for the midsummer night's dream in white. But it had worked its magic. She said, 'I've waited all my life for this to happen to me!' They hot-footed it out of town together that moment, and were in each other's arms on the nearest available woodland bank before it even occurred to them to ask each other's names.

Mother Nature, in all her moods, is a winner in this context. She is always on the side of lovers, and if you've never made mad passionate love in a forest, up a mountain, beside a lake, beneath the trees, you haven't lived — and what's stopping you? But Nature and her elements are not the absolute prerequisites for a proposition poetical. One poet, Giles Farnaby, asked his lady to imagine the perfectly unpoetical subject of a 'silly flea'. He then suggested slyly:

> *Were I a flea in bed, I would not bite you,*
> *But search some other way for to delight you.*

Ooooh yes. Well, a lover can bite a little bit — just so long as it doesn't really hurt . . .

But the mother and father of all the propositions in this vein is the number that rattled the candlesticks on every piano in the land during the Victorian period. 'Come into the garden, Maud', bearded baritones would warble passionately to bosomy beauties, 'For the black bat, Night, has flown':

> *Come into the garden, Maud,*
> *I am here — at the gate — alone!*

Who says the Victorians were repressed? It's a myth. This luscious lyric is positively aquiver with sensuality. The author, Tennyson, claimed to suffer from depression, a claim disputed by his elder brother: 'I am the *most melancholy* of the Tennysons', he would say reprovingly. But that could only have been when he wasn't cheering himself up by thinking about a bit of the other, in Les Dawsonese. For the poem swells to a climax rioting with the most colourful version of masculine sexual ecstasy that any chap could be privileged to enjoy:

> *There has fallen a splendid tear*
> *From the passion flower at the gate.*
> *She is coming, my dove, my dear;*
> *She is coming, my life, my fate!*
> *The red rose cries, 'She is near, she is near',*
> *And the white rose weeps, 'She is late' . . .*
>
> *She is coming, my love, my sweet;*
> *Were it ever so airy a tread,*
> *My heart would hear her and beat,*

> *Had I lain for a century dead;*
> *Would start and tremble beneath her feet*
> *And blossom in purple and red.*

Do you think that this is what Hemingway means in *For Whom The Bell Tolls* when he asks, 'Did the earth move? for you, too?' Tennyson, Alfred Lord, was obviously a man who could make the earth move – and that, after all, is what every woman is looking for. It helps if he looks like Paul Newman, Robert Redford, Jeremy Irons or Sting. But he doesn't have to. My best friend thinks even Richard Dreyfuss is 'kinda cute'. And all toms are grey in the dark, as every pussy knows.

Sadly, a quick blast of the poetics as a preliminary to an earth-shaking consummation is a treat reserved for all too few women. Post-Tennyson, maybe only a brave man would try it. But one who has, with considerable success, is Richard Sylvester. His poem is a witty spoof on what people reverently call 'The New Technology'. It's also a masterpiece of graceful suggestiveness – unless you want to read it literally as a hymn to his hi-fi system:

> *Electronic baby,*
> *Let me test your circuit,*
> *Let me take your valves out one by one,*
> *Blow on them,*
> *Polish them,*
> *And replace them all*
> *Individually.*
> *Let me trace your wiring . . .*
> *Let me plug you in . . .*
> *Let me switch you on . . .*
> *Electronic baby,*
> *Let me finally come*
> *Into your closed circuit.*

♡ 131 ♡

Well blow mah mind, as Scarlett O'Hara never said. If this doesn't make you crackle with desire, keep trying. With a computer future looming, women have got to be prepared for anything!

Even a robot, propositioning in poetry, is in with a chance. Most men, like Molière's *Bourgeois Gentilhomme*, have to settle for the discovery that they've been talking prose all their lives. But don't knock it. Prose is a perfectly adequate medium for some perfectly wonderful propositions, and no one demonstrates this better than Dick Francis.

Thriller king Francis is one of the most enjoyable of contemporary prose writers, though the grip of his tense yarns is such that most people don't have time to notice. His is the kind of style in which so much more is implied than ever is said.

This is exactly the way in which his heroes conduct their propositions of the ladies on whom their eyes alight, in between horses and villains and other denizens of the Francis landscape. His men are never coarse and demanding, but cool and laid-back. The DF hero knows that oblique is elegant, and a gentleman jockey does not rush his fences or expect to walk up to a strange mare and jump on. They've mastered the essential technique, of suggesting the idea in a roundabout way. This allows the girl vital room for manoeuvre, and pays her the compliment of not taking her agreement for granted.

> *Louise answered the telephone. When I told her what I wanted, she was incredulous.*
>
> *'You've actually found him?'*
>
> *'Well,' I said. 'Probably. Will you come, then, and identify him?'*
>
> *'Yes.' No hesitation. 'Where and when?'*

'*Some place in Bristol.*' *I paused, and said diffidently,* '*I could pick you up in Oxford this afternoon, and we could go straight on. We might spot him this evening . . . or tomorrow morning.*'

There was a silence at the other end . . . and then her voice, quiet and committed.

'*All right.*'

All right indeed – the perfect proposition, asking her nicely, but allowing her to say no. The DF hero is appealing in other ways, too. He's prepared to take the risk of a refusal, which the eggshell egos of so many men won't tolerate. But best of all he cares, he really cares. This is the theme of a characteristic bitter-sweet moment from *Reflex*:

'*A great day,*' *Clare said, smiling over the coffee.* '*Where's the nearest train?*'

'*Swindon. I'll drive you there . . . or you could stay.*'

She regarded me levelly. '*Is that the sort of invitation I think it is?*'

'*I wouldn't be surprised.*'

She looked down and fiddled with her coffee spoon, paying it a lot of attention. I watched the bent, dark, thinking head, and knew that if it took her so long to answer, she would go.

'*There's a fast train at ten-thirty,*' *I said.* '*You could catch it comfortably. Just over an hour to Paddington.*'

'*Philip . . .*'

'*It's all right,*' *I said easily . . .*

Needless to say, Clare isn't refusing him because she doesn't like him. In fact, she likes him so much that she wants him to know exactly why she has to say no:

'*There's a Board meeting in the office tomorrow,*' *she said.*

♡ 133 ♡

'It will be the first I've been to. They made me a Director a month ago, at the last one.'

I was most impressed, and said so. I understood, also, why she wouldn't stay. Why she might never stay. The regret I felt shocked me with its sudden intensity, because my invitation to her hadn't been a desperate plea but only a suggestion for passing pleasure. I had meant it as a small thing, not a lifetime commitment. My sense of loss, on that railway platform, seemed out of all proportion . . .

Dick Francis, of course, conjures up a quintessentially English world, of horsey men and county maidens, where any suffering is inward and the only fancied horses in the race of life run under names like Cool Customer, Grin And Bear It, and Dignity In Defeat. For the word from the American horse's mouth, what better tipster than Philip Roth? His best-selling novel *Portnoy's Complaint* is a practical handbook of what to say, who to and when, with all the variants and synonyms that you're likely to need even in a whole lifetime devoted to the hunt.

Of a zillion possibles, one of the winners must be the sequence where Portnoy meets and propositions the girl whom he later christens 'The Monkey':

. . .and then one night, on the corner of Lexington and Fifty-Second there she is, wearing a tan pants suit and trying to hail a cab — lanky, with dark and abundant hair, and smallish features that give her face a kind of petulant expression, and an absolutely fantastic ass.

Why not? What's lost? Go ahead, you shackled and fettered son of a bitch, SPEAK TO HER. She has an ass on her with the swell and cleft of the world's most perfect nectarine! SPEAK!

'Hi' — softly, and with a little surprise, as though I might have met her somewhere before . . .

'What do YOU want?'

'To buy you a drink,' I said.

'A real swinger,' she said, sneering.

Sneering! Two seconds — and two insults! To the Assistant Commissioner of Human Opportunity to this whole city!

'To eat your pussy, baby, how's that?'

My God! She's going to call a cop! Who'll turn me in to the Mayor!

'That's better,' she replied.

So a cab pulled up, and we went to her apartment, where she took off her clothes and said, 'Go ahead.'

There you are. Whatever works for you. You can't imagine the Portnoy approach going down too well in Cheltenham Spa, say, or even Sloane Square. But every chap ought to have the sense to know that when in Rome . . . So don't just stand there drooling — as the Monkey says, 'Go ahead!'

Let's Do It

A PROPOSITION CAN BE STYLISH, elegant and flowery – if you're in luck. But most men weren't cut out for scaling the heights of poetry and passion – the very idea is enough to bring on a severe attack of vertigo in the average Briton. And being a down-to-earth sort, Mr Average sees no point in beating about the gooseberry bush. If he fancies a bit of *sub rosa* at the bottom of your garden, the old Adam in him will just put it to you, thorns and all.

There's a lot to be said for the Proposition Direct. You know where you're working. A woman can often warm to a man who comes clean, and briskly suggests an interlude of workers' playtime. 'Look,' said one man to me at the end of a wearisome conference, when financial cut-backs and reorganization problems had reduced company morale to rock bottom:

> *How would you like to come to bed with me tonight? You're the most attractive woman here, I'm getting the annual award tomorrow for Salesman-Most-Likely-To – they're*

*all expecting it of us. We should do it — just to give 'em all
heart.*

Tall, well-groomed, with a fantastic lean and hungry look,
he was indeed the Man Most Likely To. Never say an
Englishwoman cannot hear the call of duty, even when it
comes sounding strangely like the call of the wild. But
pour encourager les autres? What would you have done?

Inevitably the prototype of the 'let's not mess about'
approach was D. H. Lawrence. He was always writing
ground rules for lovers. Here is one set addressed, rather
aggressively, as if to enemy rather than friend:

To Women, As Far As I'm Concerned

1. *The feelings I don't have I don't have.*
2. *The feelings I don't have, I won't say I have.*
3. *The feelings you say you have, you don't have.*
4. *The feelings you would like to have, we neither of us
   have.*

Got that, all you 'orrible little women out there? Yessir! I
can't hear yer! SAH! YESSAH!

Admittedly the rule numberings are not in the original.
But Lawrence seriously intended the whole thing this way.
Doesn't it make you wonder why anyone, particularly
women, ever rushed to join Bert's Army? Just listen to the
end of this tirade:

*So if you want either of us to feel anything at all
You'd better abandon all idea of feeling altogether.*

Geddit?
Goddit?
Good!
GEDDEMOFF!

That's the way to tell 'em.

The direct approach does not mean a man has to treat a woman like an overbearing NCO with the greenest rookie in a pack of raw recruits. He can dispense with diplomacy and still be attractive. There's a macho grace in a man with enough *cojones* to take the bull by the horns. Ben Jonson's great hero, Volpone, pinning the unsuspecting Celia to the bed, simply informs her:

> *Thou hast in place of a base husband*
> *Found a worthy lover!*

Lucky old Celia. It always strikes a woman as a weakness of this magnificent drama that Celia at this point acts so *wet*. Confronted with this thrillingly romantic figure, half man, half fox, courting her with wine and song, sensuous compliments, pearls and diamonds, all goody-goody Celia can do is pray, weep, clap her legs together and screech for help. Some opportunities are wasted on some women.

On the other hand, most propositions are not at all hard to resist. Any woman would gladly take money for every time she's heard the one that begins 'We're both adults . . .' Then there's the one solemnly recommended by US sexologist John Eichenlaub MD as guaranteed to make a woman buckle into a man's arms:

> *You are an A-1 tumblebun.*

Hop off, Eichenlaub. Corniest of all is any proposition that begins 'My wife . . .' Yukkiest of all is anything in the genre which may be called 'naming of parts'.

This is a category especially favoured by propositioning males. It's quite staggering to a woman how dearly fond men are of giving a special separate personality to their own personal private pendant — and not just 'the old man', 'the holy trinity' or 'the wife's best friend'. When you get to know men well enough to find out these things, you discover that they've all got some hysterical little nursery nickname for the biggest thing in their lives (if not the biggest in *yours*).

Choice in this depends on individual preference. 'Percy' and 'Willie' are always with us. RAF types go for 'George, the automatic pilot', 'the Red Baron', and even Biggles. One lapsed monk used to refer to his lower self as 'The Bishop', shrieking with ribald laughter. But my best was a 15-stone hunk who'd played prop-forward for Wales, and was famous up and down the valleys as a scrum in himself. The lucky girls kept a welcome in the hillsides for his 'Binkie'! Think of that next time you see Willie John McBride!

So, no matter how much they sound like Noddy in Toytown and the Blighted Enid at her worst, here are some real-life, true (honest to God!) propositions in this line:

♡ *Percy's ready to come out to play.*
♡ *Wake Willie up, shall we?*
♡ *What say we let George take over? — he'll fly us home.*

But the star award goes to the rugby player. His bid, which brought the girls running from their spinning wheels as far away as Llanfairfechan and Llandeilo consisted simply of:

Binkie wants a bite.

Doesn't set your teeth a-twitch? Try imagining it in a magical lilting Welsh accent. As said by Richard Burton, perhaps?

In fairness, even the most dreadful line *can* work. A handsome Aussie has made himself the Terror of Earl's Court with his killing parodies of the *Private Eye* gag, 'Let's uncoil the one-eyed trouser snake'. He could also pull out 'pyjama python' and the whole armoury of cod okkerisms when he felt like a textual variant.

Some men are more conscious than others that even with a Welsh lilt, a cap for Wales, and the best replacement set of false front teeth that the Land Of Your Fathers can afford, a man might not be enough in himself. In the past, especially, it was customary to accompany a proposition with the inducements thought necessary to make the lady likely to accept it. Sir Charles Dilke, the noticeably Liberal politician and famous fornicator, used to offer women *a signed photo of himself* in return for their favours!

But most men know that something more tangible than this is expected, and if it's a serious business proposition, it's going to be more than a quid pro quo. A man looking for a long-term arrangement would often fix on a particular woman, and make his proposition, just like a proposal, in full and in form. Actresses were particularly vulnerable to these approaches, as they were often unjustly held to be not as respectable as they ought to be. So they often found themselves fighting off the johnnies who weren't content to remain safely at the stage door.

A hit play of the 1850s gives us a glimpse into this vanished world. In *Masks and Faces* the leading character is the actress Peg Woffington, who had flourished as the leading female star of the stage a century earlier. Charles Reade, the author, was a close life-long friend of the actress Laura Seymour, and this love affair gave him a rare insight into what really went on behind the scenes. Here one admirer has called on La Woffington to take possession of her as his mistress:

POMANDER: *I had the honour, madam, of laying certain propositions at your feet.*

WOFFINGTON: *Oh, yes, your letter, Sir Charles. I ran my eye down it as I came along, let me see – 'A coach', 'a country house', 'pin money' – heigh ho! And I am so*

> *tired of coaches, and houses, and pins. Oh yes, here is*
> *something — what is this you offer me, up in this corner?*
> POMANDER: *That? — My heart!*

So far, so good, we may think — especially those of us who
are not exactly overwhelmed with such offers. Dorothy
Parker summed it up:

> *Why is it no-one ever sent me yet*
> *One perfect limousine, do you suppose?*
> *Oh no, it's always just my luck to get*
> *One perfect rose!*

But unfortunately Pomander himself would have to be
taken along with his goodies. And he is an odious, vain,
arrogant man. Mistress Peg wouldn't touch him with a
barge-pole, and takes an indecent delight in telling him
so:

> POMANDER: *Favour me with your answer.*
> WOFFINGTON: *(tearing the letter up) You have it.*
> POMANDER: *(aghast) Tell me, do you really refuse?*
> WOFFINGTON: *My good soul, are you so ignorant of*
> *the stage and the world, as not to know that I refuse*
> *offers such as yours every week of my life? I have refused*
> *so many of them, that I assure you I have begun to forget*
> *they are insults.*
> POMANDER: *Insults, madam! These are the highest*
> *compliments you have left it in our power to pay you.*
> WOFFINGTON: *Indeed! Oh, I take your meaning. To*
> *be your mistress could be but a temporary disgrace — to*
> *be your wife might be a lasting discredit!*

Game, set and match to Woffington in this encounter. But
perhaps the suitor had a lucky escape. In real life 'lovely
Peggy' had scores of lovers, among them small but sexy

star actor David Garrick, the Dudley Moore of the eighteenth century, and was openly unfaithful to them all. She had an actress' temperament, too. Once, in a fit of jealousy, she followed a rival actress off the stage and plunged a knife in her back! The men whose propositions she turned down generally had more to be thankful for than those who were accepted.

Nowadays, the proposition direct is more likely to be an unpretentious one-liner, than the old-style offer that sounded more like a legal contract. When the heroine has her hair blonded 'all white and silky' in *To Have And Have Not*, the Hemingway hero, perennially short on words at his best, throws around no more of the magic monosyllables than it takes to say:

> *Let's go to the hotel.*

Sometimes the proposition is slipped in unannounced, and even with a kind of innocence, like this boy-girl number from Brendan Behan's hit musical play, *The Hostage*:

SOLDIER: *I will give you a golden ball,*
To hop with the children in the hall,
TERESA: *If you'll marry, marry, marry, marry,*
If you'll marry me.
SOLDIER: *I will give you the keys of my chest,*
And all the money that I possess
TERESA: *If you'll marry, marry, marry, marry,*
If you'll marry me.
I will bake you a big pork pie,
And hide you till the cops go by,
SOLDIER: *If you'll marry, marry, marry, marry,*
If you'll marry me.
But first I think that we should see
If we fit each other —

TERESA: *(to the audience) Shall we?*
SOLDIER: *Yes, let's see.*

And they jump into bed together like two puppies in a basket, children of a divided Ireland finding a moment of peace and happiness against the never-ending backdrop of the Troubles.

The great one-line proposition isn't usually as sweet and child-like as this. But it is by way of being an undiscovered art-form of the twentieth century, practised by all manner and degree of men. Inevitably, 'would you like to come up and see my etchings' has now been superseded by the invitation to view a video. Home computers are also often kept in bedrooms, strangely enough ('I like to relax with it before I go to sleep') Well, yes. This is the age of the chip. But chips with *everything?*

Much simpler is the line with which delicious dirty Dick scores in *The Group*, Mary McCarthy's scintillating exposé of how girls lose their innocence. And the most innocent of them all *was* the well-bred Bostonian, Dottie:

> *The group would never believe, never in a million years, that Dottie Renfrew would come here, to this attic room that smelled of cooking fat, with a man she hardly knew, who made no secret of his intentions, who had been drinking heavily, and who was evidently not in love with her.*

So what's the secret? The secret is that Dick, though so dreadful, had 'fastened his deep, shadowed eyes on her', and by this simple act has produced 'a sudden harsh thump of excitement, right in *there*', which Dottie simply has to follow up, to allay the wild sexual curiosity he's evoked. So all he has to say is:

> *Do you want to come home with me?*

♡ 143 ♡

and the rest is one of the funniest, most touching and honest accounts of what happens to a girl like Dottie in the whole of modern fiction.

One-line propositions, as this shows, need not be ugly just because they're functional. Think of Elvis Presley helping an entire generation of men to stiffen the sinews, summon up the blood, and put some beef into their own approaches with the passionate urgency of 'It's now or never!'

> *Please hold me tight,*
> *Kiss me, my darling,*
> *Be mine, tonight!*

'How do you like your eggs done for breakfast?' has done good service for a charming Australian producer living on a houseboat in Little Venice. And a contemporary of John (*Reds*) Reed recalled him getting a girl into bed with the taunting question:

> *Aren't you PAGAN enough?*

And who could ever forget the one and only Clint Eastwood in *The Outlaw Josey Wales*, narrowing his eyes at the heroine and saying simply:

> *Show me!*

Clint Eastwood, unsurprisingly, both gives and gets heaps of propositions in the course of his screen capers. Often he doesn't have to say even that much – he's so magnetic that it just drops right into his lap! As he invariably plays a man who has been subjected to a severe word rationing, his propositions are not of the flowery and verbose sort. But he always avoids terrible old friends like 'your place or mine?' And he never descends to the nasties that, as every female

♡ 144 ♡

knows, are part of the local patois on every street corner in the land.

For some men specialize in what can only be called anti-propositions, the toe-curling one-liners that come like a sock in the solar plexus. Unless a woman has spent her life researching an Eskimo tribe, down an abandoned mine or up a pole on a remote hillside, she will have had any number of variants on:

♡ *How about a bit of how's your father?*
♡ *Got time for a quick one?*
♡ *If we get a move on, you can just fit me in.*
♡ *I haven't got any time to waste, do you screw?*

You get the feeling that the scum of the earth is leaving its ring around your bathtub.

New York spies report Dustin Hoffman's beautiful leggy ballet-dancer ex-wife being accosted in a lift by an ambitious homunculus with ideas above his station. 'Hi, honey?' he began,

What would you say to a little fuck?

To which, with magnificent disdain she replied:

Hello, little fuck.

That's the way to tell 'em. If it hasn't happened to you, get ready. You're overdue for your run-in with the nasty, brutish and short. Prepare some excoriating response that will blast the blister who dares to say to you, in the fragrant phraseology of one of Trevor Griffith's *Comedians*:

There's no chance of a quick shag, is there?

I ask you, who could refuse? And how would *he* like his eggs for breakfast? As a serving suggestion, straight over his head, plate and all! Go to it!

Ladies' Night

The female of the species is more deadly than the male

Rudyard Kipling

REMEMBER THE BIT IN *Bronco Billy* when the heroine rushes into Billy's bedroom and tells him that she wants him to take her in his arms and make love to her ALL NIGHT? When the hero (who else but the one and only C. Eastwood?) modestly demurs she beats down his protests and jumps on top of him. Clint is last seen going under like the *Lusitania*, slowly but with great dignity, mumbling '*Take it easy, Miss Lily!*'

This may not be quite what Jane Austen or your mother would have in mind as lady-like behaviour. But if *you* had the chance of the next half-hour in bed with Clint Eastwood (never mind the rest of your life) would you reach for the smelling salts and flee? Or would you make the kind of grab that would put an army of body-snatchers to shame? Confess, now. Don't be shy. Make a clean breast of it. Thousands of other women have led the way.

For he-Tarzan, the sexual supremo of animal power and drive, is really a myth. A gorgeous one, admittedly – how often have you waited for your bus in the rain on the Old

♡ 146 ♡

Kent Road, and fantasized that he'll come swinging down on his vine, and yodel you off to his sun-drenched jungle playground? But in real life every Jane, pretty or plain, has to do a fair bit of her own vine-swinging, drum-beating and pouncing, unless she's going to be left at the bus stop with the guy who looks like Cheetah, only not so handsome!

As with the marriage stakes, women have simply not been content to leave these important transactions in the hands of men. Liberated ladies reckon to make their own propositions, and to take their chances like men, win or lose. They're not coy about this – why should they be?

How would you like to shaft me?

is the engaging frank, no frills approach of the heroine of David Halliwell's play, *Little Malcolm*. And what could be more funny, touching and sexy than Diane Keaton in *Reds* spreading her coat on the ground, sitting down, and saying firmly to her hero:

Mr Reed, I'd like to see you with your pants off.

Meanwhile Warren Beatty looks over his shoulder, nervously hitches the pants, and tries to look as if this sort of thing happens to him all the time to the off-screen strains of 'Onward, Christian Soldiers' rising in the background.

Erica Jong, as befits one of the twentieth century's premier stylists, wraps it up a little more. Her heroine Isadora searches for the holy grail of the 'zipless fuck' through two novels, a thousand or two different men, and uncounted sexual variations some of which you've never thought of and more of which you'll never have the nerve to try (what about the champagne bottle caper, then?)

But finally she meets her heart's desire. He is The One, whatever Tolkien says. This must be why she is prepared

♡ 147 ♡

to stick at it with him. She deserves a gold star for her persistence in the teeth of the imbecilic slowness of the object of her fancy:

> *Josh and I drove round for hours . . . It was three in the morning, then it was four, then it was five. Still we were driving around . . .*
>
> *'I feel there's something unspoken here,' I blurted out (as we were riding down the deserted strip for what must have been the tenth time).*
>
> *'Unspoken?' Josh said, vaguely.*
>
> *'Possibly you want to take me to bed?' (My heart started pounding with astonishment at my own chutzpa).*
>
> *'Bed?' he said, as if he'd never heard the word before, as if the object itself were unfamiliar to him, an archaeological find, a household item from early Greece no longer in use today and unknown except to specialists.*
>
> *'Bed?' he repeated with the same stupefied air.*

Well, perhaps he had a headache. Or a shortage of *chutzpa*. It happens.

It also happens that a girl often has to take the rough with the rough when she decides to throw her knickers over the windmill. There's nothing like being madly, wildly, insanely attracted to a guy to blind you to the fact that he really is an awful toad. Or a pig. A pig especially, as in this wicked old English ballad, 'There was a lady loved a swine'. Oh yes. Don't you know the feeling?

> *There was a lady loved a swine,*
> *Honey, quoth she,*
> *Pig-hog, wilt thou be mine?*
> *Hoogh, quoth he.*
>
> *I'll build thee a silver sty,*
> *Honey, quoth she,*

> *And in it thou shalt lie,*
> *Hoogh, quoth he.*
>
> *Pinned with a silver pin,*
> *Honey, quoth she,*
> *That you may go out and in,*
> *Hoogh, quoth he.*
>
> *And wilt thou have me now,*
> *Honey, quoth she.*
> *Speak, or my heart will break —*
> *Hoogh, quoth he.*

Comes across with real feeling, that, doesn't it? Unfortunately many a swain is a swine under the skin — and you don't realize until he's got you crackling. And even if he isn't, he won't always respond to your call. That's the fate of one of the few women lucky enough to get close to a Dick Francis hero, and catch him in an unguarded moment:

> *She knocked on the way in. All the same if I'd been naked. As it was, I had my shirt off from the window cleaning, and for Honey, it seemed, that was invitation enough. She came over holding out a paper in one hand and putting the other lightly on my shoulder. She let it slide down against my skin to halfway down my back and brought it up again to the top . . .*

But Honey has drawn a blank with the hero, who wants nothing but a quiet life. He is off women in a big way, following a rocky marriage and divorce:

> *Honey sat down on the two-seater sofa and crossed her legs. She smiled. 'We haven't seen much of each other yet, have we?'*
> *'No,' I said.*

'Can I have a cigarette?'

'I'm sorry . . . I don't smoke . . . I haven't any.'

'Oh. Well, give me a drink, then.'

'Look, I really am sorry — all I can offer you is black coffee . . . or water.'

The daylight was fading fast. She came and stood close to me, not quite touching.

'You don't smoke, you don't eat, you don't drink,' she said softly. 'What else don't you do?'

'That too.'

'Not ever?'

'Not now. Not here.'

'I'd give you a good time . . .'

'Honey . . . I just . . . don't want to.'

She wasn't angry. Not even hurt. 'You're cold,' she said judiciously. 'An iceberg.'

'Perhaps.'

'You'll thaw,' she said. 'One of these days.'

But he doesn't. Or at least, not for her. For Honey it's always the big freeze. This cheerful, sensual girl does at least have the hope of getting out of the ice-age with the next warm-blooded male that comes along. Other women cannot be so casual.

Of those that dare to speak their love, not all are good-time girls looking for the next brief encounter. One of the saddest stories that Sir Thomas Malory weaves into the rich tapestry of the medieval *Morte D'Arthur* is that of Elaine, the Fair Maid of Astolat.

Elaine has had the tragic misfortune to fall hopelessly in love with Sir Lancelot — hopelessly, because he loves only Guinevere. As Lancelot is about to leave, Elaine opens her heart to him in anguish and desperation:

'My lord Sir Lancelot, now I see ye will depart; now fair

♡ 150 ♡

> *knight and courteous knight, have mercy on me and suffer me not to die for thy love.'*
>
> *'What would you that I did?' said Sir Lancelot.*
>
> *'I would have you to my husband,' said Elaine.*
>
> *'Fair damosel, I thank you,' said Sir Lancelot, 'but truly,' said he, 'I cast me never to be wedded man.'*
>
> *'Then, fair knight,' said she, 'will you be my para-mour? . . . or wit ye well, Sir Lancelot, my good days are done.'*
>
> *'Fair damosel,' said Sir Lancelot, 'of these two things you must pardon me.'*
>
> *Then she shrieked shrilly, and fell down in a swoon; and then her women bore her to her chamber, and there she made overmuch sorrow, and Sir Lancelot took his leave.*

The affecting finale to the story is well-known to all poetry-lovers from Tennyson's version of it, *The Lady of Shallot.* Elaine pines away and dies of grief, and her body is borne down the river on a barge to Camelot. There Elaine's last letter is taken from her hand for the man she loved not wisely, but too well:

> *I was your lover, that men called the Fair Maid of Astolat — pray for my soul, Sir Lancelot, as thou art peerless.*

Only a knight of Sir Lancelot's consummate chivalry could hope to extricate himself from such a delicate and poignant situation. But as the legendary champion of courtly love, he behaves with perfect honour throughout, keeping faith with his true love, but showing a tender kindness to poor Elaine. Because of this Elaine's approach to him, though bold and outspoken, retains a kind of innocence and purity quite lost in these wicked days.

And nowhere are they wickeder than in America, which has now totally displaced France as the country that uptight Brits look to for lessons in the ABC of ooh-la-la. America, kids, is Where It's At, sex-wise, liberated-woman-wise, all-wise. For as Warren Beatty enthusiastically tells Diane Keaton in *Reds*:

> *If you wanna have freedom, you gotta*
> *go where the freedom is, doncha?*

And America is *so* free — why, when a nice English girl like Julie Andrews heard Blake Edwards say she probably wore violets in her snatch, she sent him a bunch of them! Right away! Now *that* would never happen in the homeland of our own dear Queen, would it?

Julie Andrews' skilful way of turning a crack into a compliment has a lightness and wit that contrast strongly with the sexual activities of some American women — no wonder Edwards fell in love with her. Set the Andrews subtlety against that of Mrs Robinson in Charles Webb's novel *The Graduate*, who has despaired of getting her man with hints, and decides to resort to body language:

> *He turned around and was about to leave the room when Mrs Robinson stepped in through the door. She was naked.*
> *'Oh God.'*
> *She smiled at him.*
> *'Let me out,' Benjamin said. He rushed towards the door but she closed it behind her and turned the lock under the handle.*
> *'Don't be nervous,' she said.*

This is in fact a necessary instruction, as Benjamin is practically gibbering with fear — as well he might be. For Mrs Robinson is the wife of his father's business partner, they are upstairs in her bedroom, and her husband is expected home at any second. As the last straw, this is for

Benjamin what the mags coyly call The First Time. No wonder that he is in a terminal state of double-declutch:

> *'Benjamin?'*
> *'Get away from that door!'*
> *'I want to say something first.'*
> *'Jesus Christ!' Benjamin put his hands up over his face.*
> *'Benjamin, I want you to know I'm available to you,'*
> *she said. 'If you won't sleep with me this time —'*
> *'Oh my God.'*
> *'If you won't sleep with me this time, Benjamin, I want*
> *you to know you can call me up any time you want and*
> *we'll make some kind of arrangement.'*
> *'Let me out!'*
> *'Do you understand what I said?'*
> *'Yes! Yes! Let me out!'*
> *'Because I find you very attractive and any time —'*
> *Suddenly there was the sound of a car passing along the*
> *driveway under the window.*

You got it. The husband. Who else? In the movie version Dustin Hoffman, making his début as Benjamin, played this sequence with a brilliant sense of farce, just making it to the downstairs bar, ice-cubes rattling like castanets in his quivering glass, as the husband strolled in through the door.

But for the most single-minded dedication in pursuit of a shrivelling male, the no-holds-barred award goes to Saul Bellow's Angela in *Mr Sammler's Planet*. Angela is a rich creation, the all-American woman on the rampage, the US female life force at work in the city with the most life and force in the entire world, New York:

> *She crossed her legs in a chair too fragile to accommodate*
> *such thighs, too straight for her hips. She opened her purse*

*for a cigarette and Sammler offered her a light. The smoke
came from her nose, and she looked at him, when she was
in good form, with a touch of slyness. The beautiful
maiden.*

Just try mentally comparing the luscious, knowing Angela
with a Sloane Ranger, say, or one of the annual crop from
Cheltenham Ladies' College. Can't quite see Angela at a
point-to-point, can you?

*When she became hearty with him, and laughed, she
turned out to have a big mouth, a large tongue. Inside the
elegant woman he saw a coarse one. The lips were red, the
tongue was often pale. That tongue, a woman's tongue —
evidently it played an astonishing part in her free,
luxurious life.*

And he isn't complimenting her on her conversation,
either. The very name 'Angela' is one of Saul Bellow's
buried jokes, since she's no angel, but a woman with a past
that she's determined to turn into a future:

*To her first meeting with Wharton Horricker, she had come
running uptown from East Village. Something she couldn't
get out of. She had used no grass that night, only whisky,
she said. Grass didn't turn her on as she best liked turning
on. Four telephone calls she made to Wharton from a
crowded joint. He said he had to get his sleep; it was after
one a.m.; he was a crank about sleep, health. Finally she
burst in on him with a big kiss. She cried, 'We're going to
fuck all night!'*

This is the kind of conviction that makes Angela succeed
where other women have failed. She is perfectly confident
that she can bring down a moving target. She has also

obviously committed to memory the unofficial motto of the Green Berets:

> *When you've got 'em by the balls,*
> *the hearts and minds will follow.*

Such is the nature of Angela's triumph:

> *But first she had to have a bath. Because she had been longing all evening for him. Taking off everything, but overlooking the tights, she fell into the tub. Wharton was astonished and sat on the commode-cover in his dressing-gown while she, so ruddy with whisky, soaped her breasts. Sammler knew quite well how the breasts must look. Little, after all, was concealed by her low-cut dresses. So she was soaped and rinsed, and the wet tights with joyful difficulty were removed, and she was led to bed by the hand. Or did the leading. For Horricker walked behind her and kissed her on the neck and shoulders. She cried 'Oh!' and was mounted.*

US cavalry to the rescue once again? America *is* another country; they do things differently there.

III

The Real Thing

Love and marriage,
Love and marriage,
Go together like a horse and
  carriage,
This I tell you, brother,
You can't have one without the other.
            Sammy Cahn and Jimmy Van Heussen

The Heart's Desire

Let me not to the marriage of true minds
Admit impediment. Love is not love
Which alters when it alteration finds.

William Shakespeare

THE EXCITEMENT OF SEXUAL CONTACT, the thrill of making it with a new person, is one that never dies. And there's no reason why it should — *vive le sport*! But however warm, happy or memorable these love encounters are, they are not the real thing — the true, lasting closeness that everyone longs for. In marriage you can have all the fun of sex, and the joy of your 'dearest acquaintance' too, so much so that it can make everything else pale in comparison. This feeling was expressed very strongly by the novelist Edith Wharton:

> *Ah, the poverty, the miserable poverty of any love that lies outside of marriage, of any love that is not a living together, a sharing of all!*

Modern sexual freedom has highlighted the importance of marriage as a greater commitment, a higher kind of risk but a fuller reward. To want sex together is good fun, and holds out the promise of a jolly season's loving. To want marriage together is the deepest expression of caring, and promises a love that will last for all seasons. The real thing is not a passing fancy, however magically compounded of moonlight, music and musk roses — it strikes you both as the fulfilment of a lifetime's longing, and feels like coming home.

How can you tell the real thing from the convincing imitation, the heart's desire from all the other desires, the life partner from the madness of the moment? A critical test lies in the purity of the feeling itself. Love in marriage should be stronger than all other outside influences. When Hester Thrale, the widowed friend of Dr Johnson, fell in love with Gabriel Piozzi, he had everything going against him. He was poor, a humble musician, he was a Roman Catholic and he was young enough to be her son. Her entire family, and the great Doctor, set themselves to break it up. But after much misery they married, and lived in great happiness all their days, proving the strength of their love over worldly considerations.

This tried but true moral is the theme of a 'rich man, poor girl' ballad of Hester's day. In those days it seems that a maiden only had to trip down Richmond Hill, or set out for Strawberry Fair, to meet a gentleman who wanted to marry her. In this version, 'The Key Of My Heart', the maid shows the truth of her love by guiding her lover towards the one offer he can make that will win her:

> *Madam, I will give you a new lace cap,*
> *With stitching on the bottom, and frilling on the top,*
> *If you will be my bride, my joy and only dear,*
> *To walk and to talk with me everywhere.*
>
> *Sir, I will not accept of your new lace cap,*
> *With stitching on the bottom, and frilling on the top,*

I won't be your bride, your joy and only dear.
To walk and to talk with you everywhere.

The lover goes on to offer showers of rich presents, a silken gown with golden laces, a little silver bell to call up her servants when she's 'my lady'. But not all the baubles in the world can buy her love. At last he understands:

Madam, I will give you the key of my heart,
To lock it up forever, that we may never part,
If you will be my bride, my joy and only dear,
To walk and to talk with me everywhere.

Sir, I will accept of the key of your heart,
To lock it up forever, that we may never part,
I will be your bride, your joy and only dear,
To walk and to talk with you everywhere.

It's always heart-warming to see a man being led successfully through the steps of the wooing dance. Not all women take their responsibilities quite so seriously. Shakespeare 'knew a wench married in an afternoon as she went to the garden for parsley to stuff a rabbit'! And it's another story again if the man is not too committed to his proposal, in fact is quite unsure of anything he's doing on spaceship earth, a planet outside his control.

If that doesn't make you think of Woody Allen, then you haven't been to the movies. In *Annie Hall*, he is struggling with life's heavier demands — in fact he only proposes to Annie as part of his effort to 'achieve total heaviosity', as he puts it. But it's not easy. First you have to convince a woman that you mean it:

ALLEN: *I been thinking about this, and I think we should get married.*
KEATON: *Oh Alvie, come ON!*

♡ 161 ♡

Before you can convince the woman, you have to convince yourself. That's the hardest part:

ALLEN: *So you wanna get married or what?*
KEATON: *No. We're friends, and I wanna remain friends.*
ALLEN: *OK. Check, please!*

The real thing is real for two people, and the lover's call meets a whole-hearted response. One unknown lady of the Victorian period took the pains to return her answer in verse. She sent it in a hand-painted valentine to her best beloved, to accept his proposal of marriage:

> *Upon this day, one secret of my heart*
> *Till now concealed, shall truly be confessed.*
> *If there's a youth whose love I would command,*
> *To whom resign my maiden heart and hand,*
> *You are that youth to whose oft-proffered vow*
> *Of love and constancy I answer now.*
> *If still unchanged for me alone you live,*
> *Let your reply that fond assurance give.*

Touchingly, the beloved appears on the front of the card, shown receiving his valentine as a bluebird brings it to him across the waves. For he is a sailor, a real Bobby Shaftoe in tight white breeches and a blue middy jacket. Happily he survived the dangers and hardships of the seafaring life and returned safely to port, where his little poet was waiting for him after what must have been a long separation.

This is of course another criterion of the Real Thing, its ability to withstand discouragement and setback. To fall in love is the work of a minute — to stay in love is the achievement of a lifetime. There's a special poignancy in the long-deferred union of lovers who have been cruelly sundered by forces beyond their control. When it comes, it is the moment we've all been waiting for – sometimes, like Anne Elliot in *Persuasion*, for almost ten years.

This is the length of time since Anne lost her only love, Captain Wentworth. As a motherless and impressionable girl of nineteen, Anne has been forced to give him up because he was too young, without a position in the world, or money to keep a wife. But 'forced into prudence in her youth, she learned romance as she grew older'. She continues to love Wentworth deeply and hopelessly until chance throws them together again.

Inevitably it is hard for them to pick up the pieces. Still hurt by Anne's rejection, Wentworth has determined to marry another girl. But displaying the worth that Jane Austen hints at in his name, he ventures to propose again to Anne in a last desperate letter:

> *I must speak to you by such means as are within my reach. You pierce my soul. I am half agony, half hope. Tell me not that I am too late, that such precious feelings are gone for ever. I offer myself to you again with a heart even more your own than when you almost broke it, eight and a half years ago. Dare not say that a man forgets sooner than a woman, that his love has an earlier death. I have loved none but you. For you alone I think and plan.*
>
> *Have you not seen this? Can you fail to have understood my wishes? I can hardly write. I am every instant hearing something which overpowers me . . . Too good, too excellent creature! You do believe that there is true attachment and constancy among men. Believe it to be most fervent, most undeviating, in*
>
> F.W.
>
> *I must go, uncertain of my fate. But I shall return hither,*

*or follow your party, as soon as possible. A word, a look,
will be enough to decide whether I enter your father's house
this evening or never.*

As Jane Austen observes with her characteristic sweet
restraint, 'such a letter was not soon to be recovered from'.
Anne only 'recovers' from it into the kind of happiness
which she thought she had lost for ever.

This sudden, startling recognition of the bond that
makes two separate individuals into one couple is another
of the key elements of the fulfilment of the heart's desire.
Wentworth may not be every woman's ideal because as a
sailor he will have to go back to sea, and they will be
parted. Closer to a modern woman's dream is the lover,
husband, friend, with whom you can share everything,
even your work life. Mary Quant, Laura Ashley, Erica
Jong, Jane Fonda, all have husbands who understand their
work and help their careers − why not me, you think?

Obviously there's every good reason why *their* husbands
aren't helping you with *your* career! But there's no good
reason why you can't find your own Mr Siddons. Or Mr
Thatcher or Mr Streisand for this day and age.

A woman who does just that is the brave, lovable heroine
of Anne Tolstoi Wallach's recent novel, *Women's Work*. In
this story Domina has to struggle constantly against the
men in her world of work. She's an advertising executive,
twice as good at her job as any man in the outfit, but only
half as highly regarded by the short-sighted schmucks who
run it. She's fed up to the back teeth with their patronizing
attitudes, and determined to make her mark in some way
that counts.

What this comes down to for her is a series of battles,
in boardroom, bedroom, salon and sidewalk. Outnum-
bered by the dinosaurs at the top, Domina loses her battle

to make them take her seriously. But she wins the war. For en route she captures the attention of one of the enemy generals, and the guts and verve of her campaign bring him over to her side for good. After a nervewracking series of collisions and separations, he comes back to offer to fight with her, for her, alongside her:

> *'Sweetheart,' Roe said . . . 'Oh Domina, how I've missed you.' He's my home, she thought, my real home. It will never be dark and cold while he's there with me. Nothing like him has ever happened to me, couldn't happen with anyone else. He is what I will never leave . . .*
>
> *'Let's go, Domina,' said Roe. 'Partners. Best damn agency the world ever saw. I'll match you. Equal time. We'll do it piece by piece, show everyone how. My money, my training, your talent and dazzle. Partners. Say yes, say it now. I want you to say yes to me.'*

What Roe offers is a new kind of commitment, a new kind of togetherness:

> *Partners? She and Roe fitted together in work the way their bodies had fitted together just now. Marvellous. How they could match each other, she thought, how wonderfully they could act without explaining, speak each other's mind, look at each other in meetings, and know what to do next . . .*
>
> *Partners.*
>
> *We may never go home, she thought, we won't ever have to go home. If we're working together as closely as that, we'll BE home.*
>
> *That thought was so fantastic that her mind seemed to expand and fill with sparks till there was no more room, and the little sparks cascaded down her neck, her back, swirled around in her bloodstream . . .*
>
> *'Come,' she said.*

Domina and Roe's partnership is the highest kind of modern dream, where the lovers do not have to be apart for anything. But it has as its foundations a deep and shared love such as all those in love hope to build on. And however you are going to live your life, nothing can take away from the miracle of knowing that someone wants to live it with you. If you have this, you have it all — all you will ever need from now on.

How Deep Is The Ocean

'Is it possible to offer more than the most tender affection and lifelong devotion?' the young man demanded.

'It depends how we take it. It is possible to offer a few other things besides, and not only is it possible, it's usual. A lifelong devotion is measured after the fact; and meanwhile it is customary in these cases to give a few material securities. What are yours?'

Henry James, *Washington Square*

NO BOOK OF PROPOSALS would be complete without a glance at the proposal nineteenth-century style, when the offer was like the courtship itself, long and complex, the crown and glory of a deep and difficult love. The would-be husband in those days was required to come through with all good things, both emotional and material. It was not a serious offer unless a man could make it in the fullest measure.

Not all suitors were equally well supplied with both love and money, and those with a shortage of one had to rely on an abundance of the other. A lover who has more in his heart than his pocket is David Copperfield, in Dickens' ever-enchanting novel. David is head over heels

in love with Dora, who is exquisitely pretty and affection-
ate, in short perfection in all things except for her lap-dog
Jip. This petted pooch of a peevish disposition gets all the
kisses that David jealously feels are his due!

When David makes his offer, he offers his all, pouring
out his heart and soul at her feet:

> *I don't know how I did it. I did it in a moment. I*
> *intercepted Jip. I had Dora in my arms. I was full of*
> *eloquence. I never stopped for a word. I told her how I loved*
> *her. I told her I should die without her. I told her that I*
> *idolized and worshipped her. Jip barked madly all the*
> *time.*

Now it's Jip's turn to be jealous, and he does his best to get
in on the act. Fortunately David doesn't notice:

> *When Dora hung her head, and cried and trembled, my*
> *eloquence increased so much the more. If she would like me*
> *to die for her, she had but to say the word, and I was*
> *ready. Life without Dora's love was not a thing to have on*
> *any terms. I couldn't bear it and I wouldn't. I had loved*
> *her every minute, day and night, since I first saw her. I*
> *loved her at that minute to distraction. I should always*
> *love her, every minute, to distraction. Lovers had loved*
> *before, and lovers would love again; but no lover had loved,*
> *might, could, would or should love, as I loved Dora. The*
> *more I raved, the more Jip barked. Each of us, in his own*
> *way, got more mad every moment.*

But Dora knows how to reconcile this discord:

> *Well, well! Dora and I were sitting on the sofa by-and-*
> *by, quiet enough, and Jip was lying on her lap, winking*
> *peacefully at me. I was in a state of perfect rapture. Dora*
> *and I were engaged.*

The Real Thing

It's easy to see why *David Copperfield* remains the most popular of all Dickens' stories. He said himself that David was his favourite of all his 'children'. Through him Dickens told his own story – the miserable, unloved childhood, the struggle for survival, and finally the ecstatic joy of finding a girl to love.

When a man offers his all, everything depends on much all he has! Having pots and pots of it doesn't necessarily make his offer any richer in the real sense. Every woman has entertained the fantasy of being sought by a man of fabulous wealth. But when Aristotle Onassis courted Maria Callas, the result was not so much an Arabian Nights spectacular as a night at the opera, Marx brothers style.

The great tycoon may have been the man with the mazuma, but he must have been behind the door when imagination was given out. His first present to Maria was a gold bracelet with 'TMWL' engraved on it ('To Maria With Love'). It rather takes the gilt off the gingerbread to know that Tina Livanos and Jackie Kennedy in their turn both also received 'TTWL' and 'TJWL' bracelets too. Did he keep a stock of them, you can't help wondering, with the initial to be filled in whenever the moment arose?

But the best was to come. When Onassis decided to propose to La Divina, he rolled up and sang her a serenade under her window. How wonderfully romantic, you may think – as in the film *Breaking Away*, where Dave wins Kathy with an aria that delights not only her but all the other girls in her block.

But the woman in this case was the world's leading song-thrush. Callas had been partnered in grand opera by the most glorious male voices ever put on this earth to send shivers down the female spine. A man who has the breathtaking crust to offer to warble in competition with that invisible company must have a part missing some-where. 'This man has billions, you must understand,' said Callas' husband, in explanation of his appeal. Billions, maybe, but hardly where it counts!

Where it counts is in the man's ability to go on loving and caring in a way that makes his offer worth its weight in gold. In Tolstoy's *Anna Karenina*, another love story runs as a counterpoint to the principal theme of doomed love. Konstantin Levin loves Kitty, and can support his proposal with a considerable estate in the country as well as the unswerving devotion of a simple heart. But Kitty has been bewitched by the heartless rake Count Vronsky, who is later to ruin Anna Karenina's life. Even so, Levin's declaration touches Kitty far more than she would have thought:

> He glanced at her; she blushed and ceased speaking.
>
> 'I told you I did not know whether I should be here long . . . that it depended on you . . .'
>
> She dropped her head lower and lower, not knowing herself what answer she should make to what was coming.
>
> 'That it depended on you,' he repeated. 'I meant to say . . . I meant to say . . . I came for this . . . to be my wife!' he brought out, not knowing what he was saying; but feeling the most terrible thing was said, he stopped short, and looked at her . . .
>
> She was breathing heavily, not looking at him. She was feeling ecstasy. Her soul was flooded with happiness. She had never anticipated that the utterance of love would produce such a powerful effect on her. But it lasted only an instant. She remembered Vronsky.

This memory is enough to turn the scales against Levin, and Kitty refuses him. In the stormy events that follow, the two are swept apart, and suffer loneliness and heartbreak. But finally chance brings them together again at a party. Kitty is nervously playing with the chalk used for keeping the score on the green baize card table. But her eyes are 'shining with a soft light' for Levin. What follows is one of the strangest proposals on record, drawn directly from life, for it is based on Tolstoy's own proposal to his wife Sonia:

> 'Here,' he said, and he wrote the initial letters, *W,Y,T,M,I,C,N,B,D,T,M,N,O,T.* These letters meant, 'When you told me it could never be, did that mean never, or then?' There seemed no likelihood that she could make out this complicated sentence, but he looked at her as though his life depended on her understanding the words . . .
>
> 'I understand,' she said, flushing a little . . .
>
> He quickly rubbed out what he had written, gave her the chalk and stood up. She wrote, *T,I,C.N,A,D* . . .

Could you decipher this? Truly lovers do speak the language of love:

> He was suddenly radiant; he had understood. It meant, 'Then I could not answer differently'.
>
> She wrote the initial letters, *I,Y,C,F,A,F,W,H.* This meant, 'If you could forget and forgive what happened'.
>
> He snatched the chalk with nervous, trembling fingers, and breaking it, wrote the initial letters of the following phrase: 'I have nothing to forget and forgive; I have never ceased to love you.'
>
> She glanced at him with a smile that did not waver . . .
>
> He sat down and wrote a long phrase . . . he was stupefied with happiness . . . he had hardly finished writing when she read his letters, and herself wrote the answer, 'YES'.

This happiness is so unexpected, so total that Levin, like a true Russian, laughs and cries with delight. He does not know that Vronsky's selfish trifling has shown Kitty that Levin is the man she really loves. All he knows is that after miles, countries, years apart, now at last he has won 'his bliss, his life, himself – what was best in himself, what he had so long sought and longed for'. And just as in all the best love stories, 'he put his arms around her and pressed his lips to her mouth that sought his kiss'. And they do live happily ever after!

All these nineteenth-century heroes have one thing in common. They know that a proposal is a big moment, and they don't let either it or themselves down. The expectations were not only one-sided. A girl, too, was brought up to look forward to the great event, and to expect the chap to get it right. One suitor who has to be rather firmly assisted through the correct motions is Oscar Wilde's Jack in *The Importance Of Being Earnest*:

JACK: (nervously) *Miss Fairfax, ever since I met you I have admired you more than any girl . . . I have met . . . since . . . I met you.*

GWENDOLEN: *Yes, I am well aware of the fact . . . I was destined to love you.*

JACK: *You really love me, Gwendolen?*

GWENDOLEN: *Passionately!*

JACK: *Darling! You don't know how happy you've made me . . . we must get married at once. There is no time to be lost.*

But as far as Gwendolen is concerned, Jack is exhibiting the most uncouth behaviour possible. She is not ready to be his Jill without being *asked*. In full. In form. Like now. In a manner reminiscent of her famous aunt, Lady Bracknell, she undertakes the task of setting him right:

GWENDOLEN: *Married, Mr Worthing?*

JACK: *(astounded) Well . . . surely. You know that I love you, and you led me to believe, Miss Fairfax, that you were not entirely indifferent to me.*

GWENDOLEN: *I adore you. But you haven't proposed to me yet. Nothing has been said at all about marriage. The subject has not even been touched on.*

JACK: *Well, may I propose to you now?*

GWENDOLEN: *I think it would be an admirable opportunity. And to spare you any possible disappointment, Mr Worthing, I think it only fair to tell you frankly beforehand that I am fully determined to accept you.*

JACK: *Gwendolen!*

GWENDOLEN: *Yes, Mr Worthing, what have you got to say to me?*

JACK: *You know what I have got to say to you.*

GWENDOLEN: *Yes, but you don't say it!*

At last, prompted, coached, cued in and kicked up the backside, Jack manages it:

JACK: *(goes on his knees) Gwendolen, will you marry me?*

GWENDOLEN: *Of course I will, darling. How long you have been about it! I am afraid you have had very little experience in how to propose.*

JACK: *My own one, I have never loved anyone in the world but you.*

GWENDOLEN: *Yes, but men often propose for practice. All my girl friends tell me so.*

Practice is not actually essential to making an offer in full measure. But passion and persistence are. It's not enough for a man to offer a woman his all, even if his all is quite a lot, when he does it in an off-hand way. The classic 'don't mind if I don't' proposal is made by the king of the off-hand, John Wayne, in his great movie, *Stagecoach*. He has met lovely pouty Claire Trevor (playing a character of Texan *schlock* prophetically named Dallas) for the first time only an hour or two before. Prompted by one of those subterranean stirrings in a cowboy's soul, 'the Ringo Kid' suddenly says:

> *Well, well . . . I still got a ranch across the border. It's a nice place. A real nice place. Trees, grass, water. There's a cabin half built. A man could live there – with a woman. Would you go?*

She can't go straight away, natch. There's baddies to be seen to, and a man's gotta do what a man's gotta do. But hunky Wayne, with his magnificent physique and his moment of pure Wordsworth ('trees, grass, water') wins the day. And go she does!

Without a doubt modern women are getting short measure in comparison with the proposals their grand-mothers received a century before. And the maestro of them all from those days is the hero of Charlotte Bronte's prototype romance, *Jane Eyre*. Wayne's backhand is nothing to Rochester's forehand – not to mention his serve, volley, lob and smash.

Mr Rochester comes from the old world of full-blooded romance, the world of all for love, and lovers who are staunch of heart. Their fidelity, their stamina, endure through time and space. A brief summary can hardly do justice to Rochester, great lover and arch-proposer, who in the course of *Jane Eyre* proposes twice, and succeeds twice, with the same woman.

His first proposal to Jane demonstrates his artistry, his scope. No quick question-popping for him, but a deep and fervent enquiry into Jane's very soul, and his own. At first Jane resents his approach, and gets angry:

> *'Do you think, because I am poor, obscure, plain and little,*
> *I am soulless and heartless? You think wrong! I have as*
> *much soul as you — and full as much heart! . . . It is my*
> *spirit addresses your spirit; just as if both had passed*
> *through the grave, and we stood at God's feet, equal — as*
> *we are!'*
>
> *'As we are!' repeated Mr Rochester — 'so,' he added,*
> *enclosing me in his arms, gathering me to his breast,*
> *pressing his lips to my lips: 'so, Jane! . . . your will shall*
> *decide your destiny,' he said, 'I offer you my heart, my*
> *hand, and a share of all my possessions.'*

But this is only the beginning. Jane is convinced that he loves another, and is only mocking her. Passions rise so high between them that Jane burst out in a storm of tears, and they have to break apart to gather their strength for the continuation of the scene. Mr Rochester, so cool at first, begins to suffer with Jane:

> *'Am I a liar in your eyes?' he asked passionately . . .*
> *'You — you strange, you almost unearthly thing! — I love*
> *you as I love my own flesh. You — poor and obscure, and*
> *small and plain as you are — I entreat you to accept me as*
> *a husband . . . You, Jane, I must have you for my own —*
> *entirely my own. Will you be mine? Say yes, quickly.'*
>
> *His face was very much agitated and very much flushed,*
> *and there were strong workings in the features, and strange*
> *gleams in the eyes.*

For Rochester, the proposal is an act of passion in itself. He lays siege to Jane, beats down her resistance with surge upon surge of emotion, and finally makes her his in a sublime fusion of sexuality and romance:

'Gratitude?' he ejaculated wildly – 'Jane, accept me quickly. Say, Edward – give me my name – Edward – I will marry you.'

'Are you in earnest? Do you truly love me? Do you sincerely wish me to be your wife?'

'I do; and if an oath is necessary to satisfy, I will swear it.'

'Then, sir, I will marry you.'

'Edward – my little wife!'

'Dear Edward!'

'Come to me – come to me entirely now,' said he; and added in his deepest tone, speaking in my ear as his cheek was laid on mine, 'Make my happiness – I will make yours.'

'God pardon me!' he subjoined ere long; 'and man meddle not with me: I have her, and I will hold her.'

Which in the end, in fullest measure, he does.

Coup De Foudre

Some enchanted evening
You will see a stranger,
You will see a stranger
Across a crowded room —

Oscar Hammerstein II

COUP DE FOUDRE — the English don't even have a word for this feeling, when quite unexpectedly and with maximum force you are struck so powerfully with the perfections of A. N. Other that you know things will never be the same again. This is the time when you pine for him by day and night; you forget to eat but drink twice as much as usual; you treasure up mementos of him to the extent of carrying round scraps of his handwriting and mooning over them twenty times a day ('Phone Jackson', 'new sox', 'Mother's b.day' can be food for love when the appetite is huge enough).

And this is the feeling which some lovers seek immediately to turn into marriage, for what could be a stronger basis for a life-time union? In a sudden flash-bang-wallop of recognition you know that this is the one person you want to spend the rest of eternity with. It's just like being silently sand-bagged behind the ear, and when it happened to me on the very first occasion I ever entered a man's college at Oxford, I thought the bells I heard ringing were just part of the normal daily concert in the city of dreaming spires.

Under the stress of this unexpected self-discovery, a man can do strange things. He can completely surprise himself as well as his beloved by an action which can change his life at a stroke. The victim, or rather the hero, of just such a wild joyful impulse is Denry Machin in Arnold Bennett's *The Card*.

Denry is a young man who has 'got on in the world', but he is rather smarter at business than at personal relationships. He is about to be well and truly caught by a designing young widow who is after his 'dibs'. But he has always had a strong feeling for Nellie, the daughter of a family who are about to emigrate. Denry goes to see them all off at the dock. As he is bidding them goodbye, something quite unexpected happens:

His eye caught Nellie's. She had not moved. He felt then as he had never felt in his life. No, absolutely never. Her sad, her tragic glance rendered him so uncomfortable and yet so deliciously uncomfortable, that the symptoms startled him. He wondered what had happened to his legs. He was not sure he had legs.

However, he demonstrated the existence of his legs by running up to Nellie . . . 'What am I doing here?' he asked of his soul . . .

And in a sort of hysteria he seized her long thin hand and dragged her along the deck to another gangway, down whose steep slope they stumbled together . . .

Nellie burst into tears. 'What are you going to do with me?' she whimpered.

'Well, what do YOU think? I'm going to marry you, of course . . .'

♡ 178 ♡

The Real Thing

> '*You can't think how you've staggered me,*' said she.
> '*You can't think how I've staggered myself,*' said he.

But neither of the newly-made couple has any doubts:

> *It was the bare truth that he had staggered himself. But he had staggered himself into a miraculous, ecstatic happiness. She had no money, no clothes, no style, no experience, no particular gifts. But she was she. And when he looked at her, calmed, he knew that he had done well for himself. He knew that if he had not yielded to that terrific impulse he would have done badly for himself.*

The transforming power of the marriage proposal is so great that lovers want to make this statement even if it is likely to be their last act on earth. This is the situation at the end of one of Bogart's great movies, *The African Queen*. As the rough, tough riverboat captain, Charlie Allnutt, Bogart has taken a strictly functional view of women. He's been in the habit of treating a female the way he treats 'the old girl' *African Queen* herself, on the 'spit into her engine, kick her in the slats, show her who's boss' principle.

But that's before he is awakened to the way it ought to be, by Katharine Hepburn's Rosie. Hepburn, never lovelier, gives him a vision of their life together which he expresses simply as:

> *You at the tiller, me at the engine — just like it was at the start.*

But before he can say 'schweetheart' they are caught by the Germans and about to be hanged as spies. In a flash, Allnutt/Bogie rises to his finest flight:

> *Captain, will you grant us a last request? Marry us! We want to get married!*

♡ 179 ♡

And by the powers invested in sea captains to match and dispatch, he does. And if you don't know that this weird and wonderful couple, *both* now all nuts, are spared to live happily ever after, then you weren't among the millions who voted this the movie they'd most like to see again on television!

Men aren't the only ones who can transform their lovers' lives from misery to bliss in an unhoped-for second. A female who successfully practises the art is Maud, the ripping, spiffing, absolutely top-hole heroine of P. G. Wodehouse's *A Damsel In Distress*. Maud has yielded to the siren call to Come Into The Garden, like her namesake of Tennyson's fevered fancy. There she meets handsome George, and love blossoms between them.

But Maud has already given her heart to another — the course of true love never did run smooth, as the sublime Jeeves might be heard to observe. It takes some very rum business, with an assortment of chumps, twerps and silly asses all teetering on the banana skin of life, to demonstrate to her that her perfect pash and former lover is, in short, a bit of a blighter.

Maud has persisted with this undeserving hound in the teeth of family disapproval — bally mess all round, ice forming on the upper slopes of the aged female relations — while unknown to her the bounder has been getting horribly fat, and trifling with a chorus girl under the beastly pseudonym of 'Pootles'. Meanwhile she has administered the old heave-ho to her true love, who like a good egg knows no better than to take no for an answer. Deuced tragic, what? In the final yoicks and tantivy of the hunt, Maud has to stand up in her stirrups to see over the pack, gather up the reins and deliver the view halloo herself, loud and clear.

The rejected swain is broken-heartedly packing for a

slow boat to China when he receives this unexpected blast
on the blower:

> '. . . George, I wanted to ask you one or two things. In the
> first place, are you fond of butter? . . . And what about
> the wallpaper in your den?'
>
> George pulled himself together . . . 'I don't understand.'
>
> 'How stupid of you! I was asking what sort of wall-
> paper you would like in your den after we are married and
> settled down.'
>
> George dropped the receiver . . . 'You said something
> about getting married.'
>
> 'Well, aren't we going to get married? Our engagement
> is announced in the Morning Post.'

This is almost too much for George, whose side of the
dialogue is already far from sparkling. Now he is reduced
to incoherence, and Maud has to pull out all the organ
stops to get the required surge:

> 'But – But –'
>
> 'George!' Maud's voice shook. 'Don't tell me you are
> going to jilt me!' she said tragically. 'Because if you are,
> let me know in time, as I shall want to bring an action for
> breach of promise . . . Will you marry me?'
>
> George yelped excitedly. 'And you really think – You
> really want – I mean, you really want – You really
> think –'
>
> 'Don't be so incoherent!'
>
> 'Maud!'
>
> 'Well?'
>
> 'Will you marry me?'
>
> 'Of course I will!'
>
> 'Gosh!'

Splendid, eh? Bright chap, George – quick on the uptake, doncher know. What ho! That'll be all, Jeeves.

Wodehouse's is the lovingly-evoked but now vanished world of the 1920s, of flappers and bright young things and comfortable certainties like bread and butter and honey still for tea. But whatever world you live in, marriage, even the offer of it, means an enormous wrench in parting from the life that late you led. It means an act of self-discovery and of self-definition that can amount to a new version of life in the future.

Nothing but the deepest love will encourage people to make these major life adjustments, often at some personal cost. The lover, in Yeats's phrase, 'has spread his dreams under your feet', given you his life to remake as the better half of yours, as in this touching lyric, *The Gypsy's Proposal*:

> *I, the man with red scarf,*
> *Will give thee what I have, this last week's earnings.*
> *Take them, and buy thee a silver ring,*
> *And wed me, to ease my yearnings.*
>
> *For the rest, when thou art wedded,*
> *I'll wet my brow for thee*
> *With sweat, I'll enter a house for thy sake,*
> *Thou shalt shut doors on me.*

This unusual poem from D. H. Lawrence's pen reflects obliquely on his own situation. Like many men Lawrence both longed for the closeness unique in marriage, and yet feared the constraint of its bonds.

A very human story of a man's ambivalence, hesitating on the threshold of this great moment and undecided whether to go forward or back, is that of Jack Benny's courtship. His girl loved him and had given him every sign of her feelings. When he told her that he was leaving town, she blurted out, 'If you were a gentleman, you'd ask me to go along with you!'

The effect that this simple line produced was devastating. The great comedian, who had this effect on so many other people, himself literally fell on the floor and rolled around, laughing his head off. Naturally somewhat miffed, our heroine lost no time in getting herself engaged to another man. But as soon as her engagement was made public, she says:

> . . . *the phone rang. It was Jack. 'I hear you're getting married.'*
>
> *'Yes, I am,' I replied.*
>
> *'Well . . . the last month or so, I've been thinking about you . . . And if ever I WANTED to get married, I'd like to marry you . . . But I DON'T want to get married . . .'*
>
> *'Well, that's fine for YOU,' I said sarcastically, 'but I'M getting married!'*
>
> *'Look,' Jack went on . . . 'I really do think you're much too young to get married . . . But if you ARE going to get married, why don't you marry me?'*
>
> *Without missing a beat, I said, 'Fine.'*
>
> *'Well then,' Jack said, 'let's get married this Friday — BEFORE I CHANGE MY MIND!'*

Happily this marriage turned out to be both long and joyful. As a husband Benny found the confidence that had escaped him as a lover. Nevertheless, love is undoubtedly easiest for the young, innocent and pure in heart. Sophisticated lovers can have a hard time abandoning themselves to the experience.

A loving couple who are acutely conscious of the moment of passage from 'I' to 'we' are Congreve's Millamant and her lover Mirabell in *The Way Of The World*. They move in the fashionable high society of eighteenth-century London, a world of amorous intrigue and cynical double dealing. In their circle, gallants and fops ruthlessly pursue the ladies for sexual favours, and a romance is something childish and naive. Both of them wish to love and be loved, but cannot endure to lose status in the cool, brittle, brilliant world of which they are the stars. They must find the recipe for adjustment, make the act of redefinition, while still remaining fashionable.

The scene in which they negotiate their marriage is one of the best-loved moments in English drama, not so much a proposal as a legal contract. Mirabell has loved Millamant so long in vain, that he can hardly credit that he is on the brink of success. Millamant is frightened of the strength of her feeling for him, and determined for pride's sake not to show the extent of his power over her:

MIRABELL: . . . *You can fly no further.*

MILLAMANT: *I'll fly and be followed to the last moment; though I am on the very verge of matrimony, I expect you should solicit me as much as if I were wavering at the gate of a monastery, with one foot over the threshold! . . . Ah, I'll never marry, unless I am first made sure of my will and pleasure.*

MIRABELL: *Would you have 'em both before marriage? Or will you be content with the first now, and stay for the other till after grace?*

MILLAMANT: *Don't be impertinent! My dear liberty, shall I leave thee?*

With this pertinent question, the couple get down to the serious business of the proposal, the negotiation of the terms on which they can live together. Millamant bans all endearments, like 'Joy, Jewel, Love, Sweetheart, and the rest of that nauseous cant with which men and their wives are so fulsomely familiar'. She insists on protecting in her marriage all the freedoms that she has enjoyed as a single woman. Her idea of how to do it is 'to be as strange as if we had been married a great while, and as well-bred as if we were not married at all'.

If all her conditions are met, Millamant feels that she may, 'by degrees, dwindle into a wife'. Mirabell responds to her teasing by asserting his determination to grow into a close and loving husband. He forbids all intrigues, gossip, whispers and scandal with women friends who would 'screen her affairs under their countenance' — he's not going to share her with other men. He also expresses a violent dislike of contemporary cosmetics — 'hog's bones, hare's gall, pig water and the marrow of a roasted cat', he calls them — she's lovely enough as she is. And finally he looks forward with gusto to when she 'shall be breeding, which may be presumed as a blessing on our endeavours'.

The very mention of pregnancy to fashion-conscious Millamant is enough to produce a fit of the vapours. Fortunately her friend enters at the critical point:

MILLAMANT: *Fainall, what shall I do? Shall I have him? I think I must have him.*

FAINALL: *Ay, ay, take him, what should you do?*

MILLAMANT: *Well, then — I'll take my death I'm in a horrid fright — Fainall, I shall never say it — well — I think — I'll endure you.*

FAINALL: *Fie, fie, have him, and tell him so in plain terms; for I'm sure you've a mind to him.*

MILLAMANT: *Are you? I think I have — and the horrid man looks as though he thought so too — well, you ridiculous thing, I'll have you — I won't be kissed nor I won't be thanked — here, kiss my hand, though — so, hold your tongue now, don't say a word.*

'Don't say a word' — how long can this silence last with

such a supremely witty and talkative pair? These two are not destined for a quiet and peaceful marriage. Yet there are many ways for people to be happy, and a mutual delight in one another's conversation lasts longer than many things that bring a couple together. And no one has ever said that only mutes are allowed to apply for the Dunmow Flitch!

The Triumph Of Love

Love is enough, though the world be a-waning,
And the woods have no voice but the voice of
*   complaining,*
Though the sky be too dark for dim eyes to discover,
The gold-cups and daisies fair blooming thereunder,
Though the hills be held shadows and the sea a dark
*   wonder,*
And this day draw a veil over all deeds passed over,
Yet their hands shall not tremble, their feet shall not
*   falter,*
The void shall not weary, the fear shall not alter
These lips and these eyes of the loved and the lover.

William Morris

'LOVE IS ENOUGH' – how much we all want this to be true! There's a special magic in the stories of love that succeed in the face of setback and suffering, triumphant over all the obstacles that are placed in its way. Every love that succeeds has to beat down at least some opposition. I had to go in fear and trembling to a Principal who could have doubled for Medusa, to ask for 'permission to get engaged'. This was a rigid rule of the college, which produced some ironical results when the 'young ladies' could get everything-else-unrespectable, but could be refused permission to accept the one suggestion that would make honest women out of them!

Then there were the weeks of weeping and wailing and gnashing of teeth when an otherwise mild pater greeted the news of The World's Greatest Marriage Proposal (mine) with the strangled cry, 'Don't tell anybody!'

This was followed up with the frosty observation, 'I never thought a daughter of mine would marry a *foreigner*', just because the Best Beloved happened at a distant point in his past to have had connections with the principality of Wales. You can't help feeling that this was not what Earl Spencer said to Lady Diana.

But the real obstacles are far more profound than petty regulations, or a pa that soon comes round as nice as pie. A cruel combination of odds-against occurs in O'Neill's powerful drama, *Anna Christie*. An Irish seaman, Burke, has fallen in love with the heroine, against the fanatical opposition of her father, an ignorant Swedish immigrant. Burke knows that he must take on the old man before he can speak to Anna herself:

> BURKE: *I'm thinking I'll take this chance while we're alone to have a word with you. And that word is soon said. I'm marrying your Anna before this day is out, and you might as well make up your mind to it whether you like it or no.*
>
> CHRIS: *Ho-ho! Dat's easy for say!*
>
> BURKE: *You mean I won't? Is it the like of yourself will stop me, are you thinking?*
>
> CHRIS: *Yes, I stop it, if it comes to the vorst.*
>
> BURKE: (with scornful pity) *God help you!*
>
> CHRIS: *But ain't no need for me to do dat. Anna —*

The old man's enigmatic utterance proves prophetic. Anna enters, and Burke asks her for her love:

BURKE: *I told him in his teeth I loved you . . . I told him I thought you had a bit of love for me, too. Say you do, Anna! Let you not destroy me entirely, for the love of God!*

ANNA: *Maybe I do. I been thinking and thinking — I didn't want to, Mat, I'll own up to that — I tried to cut it out — but — I guess I can't help it anyhow . . . Sure I do! Sure I love you, Mat!*

BURKE: *God be praised!*

ANNA: *And I ain't never loved a man in my life before, you can always believe that — no matter what happens.*

BURKE: *Sure I do be believing ivery word you iver said or iver will say. And 'tis you and me will be having a grand, beautiful life together, till the end of our days!*

OVERCOME BY A FIERCE IMPULSE OF PASSIONATE LOVE, THEY KISS. ANNA PUSHES HIM AWAY FROM HER WITH A BROKEN LAUGH.

ANNA: *Goodbye.*

Unknown to Burke, Anna has worked as a prostitute at an earlier stage of her life. She feels that to marry would be to take advantage of a good man. Now he knows she loves him, he cannot accept her refusal yet when at last she tells him, it is his turn to recoil from the idea of marriage. But their love proves strong enough to defeat the odds, and they are reconciled at the end:

BURKE: *I'm loving you in spite of it all, and wanting to be with you . . . I'd go mad if I'd not have you . . . We'll be wedded in the morning, with the help of God. We'll be happy now, the two of us, in spite of the divil!*

Lovers always have some secrets to forgive each other, though not usually ones as dark as this. More often the barriers that keep the lovers asunder are those of money and position, with much more on one side than another. This is such a perennial problem that the theme goes all the way back to the dawn of courtship. It crops up in a sweet old English ballad that was ancient in Shakespeare's day, *The Blind Beggar of Bednal Green*.

This cheerful ditty deals with an old blind beggar of London, and his 'fair daughter', Bessee. The lucky girl receives not one but *four* proposals in the course of the action, which makes you feel that there ought to be a central marriage clearing house, where proposals that are surplus to requirement could be redistributed among those who are not exactly overburdened with offers!

For Bessee is quite inundated with suitors:

'If that thou wilt marry with me,' quoth the knight,
'I'll make thee a lady with joy and delight;
My heart is enthralled with thy fair beauty,
Then grant me thy love, my dear pretty Bessee.'

The gentleman said, 'Come marry with me,
In silks and in velvets my Bessee shall be;
My heart lies distracted, oh hear me,' quoth he,
'And grant me thy love, my dear pretty Bessee.'

'Let me be thy husband,' the merchant did say,
'Thou shalt live in London most gallant and gay;
My ships shall bring home rich jewels for thee,
And I will for ever love pretty Bessee.'

But words and vows are oaths written on water. As soon as they find out what her father does for a living, her suitors drop away from her like fruit from a tree. All except one:

'Why then,' quoth the knight, 'hap better, hap worse,
I weigh not true love by the weight of the purse,
And beauty is beauty in every degree,
Then welcome to me, my dear pretty Bessee.'

Just as in a fairy-tale, it all comes right in the end. Virtue is not its only reward. For the despised daughter of the poor beggar proves to be a rich heiress, as her father showers her with the gold he has amassed from years of high-powered begging. So the story has a happy ending, with 'fair Bessee matched to her knight . . . With marvellous pleasure and wished-for delight'.

Give or take the showers of gold in the last reel, this story is the very stuff of happy-ending romances. It's the theme that links the twentieth century with the tenth and even earlier, and lies behind world-famous successes as different as *Love Story* and *The Sound of Music*. As the former shows, the happy ending is not always a happy *ever after* – hands up anyone who didn't cry over *Love Story* – when, having defeated all the other stumbling-blocks, the lovers are beaten by the last great enemy, death.

But, ideally, love should not only triumph but live to enjoy its triumph, especially when it has been won at some cost. Elizabeth Bennet and Mr Darcy manage to defeat both 'pride' and 'prejudice' in Jane Austen's novel of that name. Mr Darcy is gifted with 'a fine tall person, handsome features, and noble mein', and I hope you don't think it's vulgar to mention his ten thousand a year as well. Elizabeth is lovely, spirited and witty, and if any girl deserves Darcy and his wherewithal (apart from you or me) she does. The reader is dying for them to get it together. But there are problems . . .

Mr Darcy is verily the stuff that dreams are made of, being tall, dark and handsome but, above all, aloof. And thereby hangs a trial. For though there is nothing like a loof or two to drive women wild, Mr Darcy loofs it to excess. He's so cold and distant that when he first pays his addresses to Elizabeth, she still thinks he hates her; and what's more, she doesn't even know his first name.[1]

Now perhaps this not need be a bar to *marriage à la mode* — Elizabeth's own mother is still calling her father 'Mr Bennet' after twenty-five years of the blest condition, *and* five offspring. But the dislike factor, at first warmly entertained on both sides, is a more serious impediment. In fact it's a proper turnpike in the path of true love, and at his first attempt to hurdle it, Darcy comes a cropper and measures his length.

Or rather, Elizabeth measures it for him. Could any woman warm to a proposal that like Mr Collins's, dwells more feelingly on the reasons *against* it than the reasons *for*? 'In vain have I struggled,' he begins, 'my feelings will not be repressed. It will not do.' And away he goes, with his 1001 reasons why he shouldn't love or marry her.

What follows is what the politicians call a frank interchange of views. In this well-bred but full-blooded shemozzle, Elizabeth really cuts Darcy down to size. As she is the first person in his life ever to have done so, this serves to confirm his feeling that she is the only woman in the world for him. And in his shock and distress at her reproaches, Elizabeth perceives in him finer qualities than she has given him credit for. The love between them stirs and quickens even as they are both angrily agreeing that It Can Never Be.

Oh but it can! With her effortless skill Jane Austen sets up a series of incidents in which Darcy unlearns his pride, and Elizabeth outgrows her prejudice. He is too much of a gentleman to bear resentment, and she is too much of a

1. But then, few do. A crate of bubbly, a gold star or purple heart to anyone who knows — really *knows* — that Mr Darcy's first name is — ooh! — yes — aaah! — wait for it — *Fitzwilliam*! (sigh . . .). Follow that, Cartland, Mills and Boon and Co!

woman not to let her heart rule her head. When the chance comes to help Elizabeth's family in distress, Mr Darcy takes it by stealth. But Elizabeth finds out, and the sequel is what we have been hoping for all along, all the sweeter for being the second time around:

> '*Let me thank you again and again,*' *said Elizabeth,* '*in the name of all my family, for that generous compassion that induced you to take so much trouble . . .*'
>
> '*If you will thank me,*' *he replied,* '*let it be for yourself alone . . . your FAMILY owes me nothing. Much as I respect them, I believe I thought only of YOU.*'
>
> *Elizabeth was much too embarrassed to say a word. After a short while her companion added,* '*You are too generous to trifle with me. If your feelings are still what they were last April, tell me so at once. MY affections and wishes are unchanged; but one word from you will silence me on the subject for ever.*'

Elizabeth is almost overcome with surprise and joy at this moment. But she breathes the one word of acceptance, not rejection, with a most wondrous effect:

> *The happiness which this reply produced was such as he had probably never felt before; and he expressed himself on the occasion as sensibly and as warmly as a man violently in love can be supposed to do.*
>
> *Had Elizabeth been able to encounter his eye, she might have seen how well the expression of heart-felt delight, diffused over his face, became him; but though she could not look, she could listen, and he told her of feelings, which, in proving what importance she had for him, made his affection every moment more valuable.*

Oh yes. Isn't that just right? Port after storm, calm after troubled seas . . . the way it ought to be. Man unto woman, woman unto man, the rhythm of life since life began.

Perhaps it is not love but life itself that triumphs in bringing a man and a woman together. A profound believer in what he called 'the Life Force' was dramatist and philosopher George Bernard Shaw. To Shaw the Life Force was powerful enough to cut through any opposition, because it operates on the level where instincts say 'yes' even when will and reason resist with a resounding 'no!'

John Tanner in Shaw's *Man And Superman* certainly offers some . . . resistance to the process:

TANNER: *Ann: I will not marry you. Do you hear? I won't, won't won't, won't WON'T marry you.*

ANN: (placidly) *Well, nobody axd you, sir she said, sir she said. So that's settled . . . If you don't want to be married, you needn't be.*

TANNER: *We do the world's will, not our own. I have a frightful feeling that I shall let myself be married because it is the world's will that you should have a husband . . . But why me? Me of all men? . . . I shall decay like a thing that has served its purpose and is done with; I shall change from a man with a future to a man with a past; I shall see in the greasy eyes of all the other husbands their relief at the arrival of a new prisoner to share their ignominy. The young men will scorn me as one who has sold out: to the women I, who have always been an enigma and a possibility, shall be merely somebody else's property — and damaged goods at that — a second-hand man at best!*

But the laddie doth protest too much, methinks. As Ann in her wisdom knows, the hardest task in a woman's life is to prove to a man that his intentions are serious. Tanner loves her. He needs her. Ann concentrates all her magic to convince him that they were destined for each other . . .

ANN: *From the beginning — from our childhood — by the Life Force.*

TANNER: *I will not marry you. I will not marry you.*

ANN: *Oh, you will, you will.*

TANNER: *I tell you, no, no, no.*

ANN: *I tell you, yes, yes, yes.*

TANNER: *No . . .*

ANN: *I made a mistake: you do not love me.*

HE SEIZES HER IN HIS ARMS

TANNER: *It is false: I love you. The Life Force enchants me: I have the whole world in my arms when I clasp you . . .*

ANN: *Take care, Jack: if anyone comes while we are like this, you will have to marry me.*

TANNER: *If we two stood now on the edge of a precipice, I would hold you tight and jump!*

And this, in effect, he does. He takes the plunge. Ann finally prevails against Jack's inflated ego, his oversized hopes and fears, and proves to him that this larger-than-Life Force is twice as natural. She gets herself well and truly engaged to Tanner in spite of all!

Handsome, charming, and a devilish good talker, Tanner is privileged in every respect, as well as being what Shaw calls an M.I.R.C. (Member of the Idle Rich Class). The breakthrough of love seems even more moving and important when it happens to someone who is none of these things — someone whose expectations are so low, that the block to loving that they have to overcome is the enemy within.

The classic no-hoper who learns to love and to hope is

Paddy Chayefsky's *Marty*, the ordinary little man so memorably brought to life by Ernest Borgnine in the film of that name. Chayefsky himself said something that could apply to all lovers, 'little lives are big lives to the people who lead them'. As Marty explains himself:

> *Sooner or later there comes a point in a man's life when he gotta face some facts, and one fact I gotta face is that whatever it is that women like, I ain't got it. I chased enough girls in my life. I went to enough dances. I got hurt enough. I don't wanna get hurt no more.*

So Marty hangs around with another man on the loose, his buddy Angie, until by chance he meets a girl who really likes him. He likes her, too. But at the first sign that this could be serious, Marty's mother takes against her, and Angie weighs in to keep Marty to himself. 'She's a *dog*,' he says viciously. 'Brush her.'

This jealousy combines with Marty's own life-long sense of inferiority. We know he will let her go, and lose his one chance of happiness. But, single-handed, Marty breaks through the barriers of his own self-doubt, Angie's hostility, and the powerful drag of his male 'friends':

MARTY: *What am I, crazy or something? I got something good! What am I hanging around with you guys for?*
ANGIE: (shocked) *Watsa matter with you?*
MARTY: *You don't like her. My mother don't like her. She's a dog, and I'm a fat, ugly little man. All I know is I had a good time last night. I'm gonna have a good time tonight. If we have enough good times together, I'm going down on my knees and beg that girl to marry me. You don't like her, that's too bad.*

HE MOVES TO THE PHONE TO CALL HIS GIRL, THEN TURNS BACK TO ANGIE WITH A SMILE

♡ 196 ♡

The Real Thing

When you gonna get married, Angie? You're thirty-four years old. All your kid brothers are married. You oughtta be ashamed of yourself!

STILL SMILING AT HIS PRIVATE JOKE, HE PUTS THE DIME INTO THE SLOT AND THEN — WITH A DETERMINED FINGER — HE BEGINS TO DIAL

FADE OUT

THE END

Roses, Roses, Roses

I am the rose of Sharon, and the lily of the valleys.
As the lily among the thorns, so is my love among the daughters.
As the apple tree among the trees of the wood, so is my beloved among the sons.
He brought me to the banqueting house, and his banner over me was love.
My beloved is mine, and I am his; he feedeth among the lilies.

The Song of Songs

FALLING IN LOVE IS PROBABLY the most individual thing that any of us can do. So it's not surprising that the expression of love as marriage can take so many different forms. All lovers want their moment of union to be blessed by that special sense of something unique, romantic and magical. Yet there are so many varieties and versions of what that is, and how lovers get there. Let me finally celebrate the richness and individuality of the ways in which this moment has been achieved.

This peak has been scaled so many times in life and literature that it is almost impossible to say which are 'the best' out of all the wide range of marriage proposals in the world. Everyone must have their personal favourites, and their own experience obviously comes high up on the scale. But I hope that some of the proposals that follow would be on anyone's list of moving moments.

As they show, the marriage proposal is not just a moment of delight. It has been the vehicle for the depiction of every shade of human emotion. It has furnished writers with the material for every kind of drama from comedy through to tragedy, and can be enjoyed on a number of levels all at once.

One sure-fire winner shows that you don't have to be the veteran of lots of proposals yourself in order to dream up a real stunner. This piece, written with what one critic called a combination of 'careless power and unholy rapture', was composed when the authoress was only nine years old:

Ethel he murmered in a trembly voice.

Oh what is it said Ethel hastily sitting up.

Words fail me ejaculated Bernard horsly my passion for you is intense he added fervently. It has grown day and night since I first beheld you.

Oh said Ethel in supprise I am not prepared for this and she lent back against the trunk of the tree.

Bernard placed one arm tightly around her. When will you marry me Ethel he uttered you must be my wife it has come to that I love you so intensly that if you say no I shall perforce dash my body to the brink of yon muddy river he panted wildly.

Oh dont do that implored Ethel breathing rarther hard.

Then say you love me he cried.

Oh Bernard she sighed fervently I certinly love you madly you are to me like a Heathen god she cried looking at his manly form and handsome flashing face I will indeed marry you.

How soon gasped Bernard gazing at her intensly.

♡ 199 ♡

As soon as possible said Ethel gently closing her eyes.
My Darling whispered Bernard and he seized her in his
arms we will be marrid next week.
Oh Bernard muttered Ethel this is so sudden.

This is of course the unmistakable prose of little Daisy
Ashford, showing the truth of J. M. Barrie's claim that
The Young Visiters is 'a scrumptious affair and fit to make
all right people jump with joy'. For young Daisy already
knew what some people spend a whole life-time missing,
that everyone is longing for love and passion, for a *folie à
deux*, for emotional adventures and wild escapades under a
tree beside a river.

Some couples, however, have a harder time going with
the flow than others. And love is not always expressed in
sweet harmony, moonlight and magnolia blossom. Chek-
hov's brilliantly funny play *The Proposal* tells the story of
lovers who only find each other through the dynamic of
discord, like Katharine and Petruchio in *The Taming of
The Shrew*.

This particular prickly pair are Ivan Vassilievitch
Lomov and Natalia Stepanova. Lomov's proposal gets off
to a wonderfully comic and ridiculous start when he
presents himself one morning at Natalia's house absurdly
rigged out in white tie and tails. His unaccustomed
finery and nervous manner make her father jump to the
wrong conclusion: 'He's come to ask for money! I shan't
give him any!'

Despite his nerves, Lomov manages to declare his
purpose – he has come to make an offer, not a demand.
This produces a killing change of heart in the father,
Choobukhov:

*My dearest chap! . . . I've wished it for a long time. It
has always been my wish.* (He sheds a tear) *I've always*

♡ 200 ♡

The Real Thing

> *loved you as if you were my own son, my dearest fellow! May God grant you love and sweet concord, and all the rest of it!*

But the father is more easily won than the daughter, and love and sweet concord are not so easily come by. Before Lomov has a chance to say what he has come for, the two fall into a violent quarrel, and Natalia sends him packing with a whole earful of fleas. Then she learns from her father that Lomov had called to propose to her:

NATALIA: *To me? A proposal? Oh! Bring him back! Bring him back! Oh, bring him back!*

CHOOBUKHOV: *Bring who back?*

NATALIA: *Be quick, be quick. I feel faint. Bring him back.*

SHE SHRIEKS HYSTERICALLY

CHOOBUKHOV: *What is it? What do you want? What misery! I'll shoot myself! I'll hang myself! They've worn me out!*

NATALIA: *I'm dying! Bring him back! BRING HIM BACK!*

Lomov is hauled back in a virtual state of collapse. Natalia is now so jumpy that she can't think how to get him going again on his offer of marriage. The tension explodes into another row, about their dogs this time. The strain is too great for poor Lomov, and he faints. Natalia is convinced that she's lost him again, and goes off into a major fit of screaming hysterics. It's left to the father, not himself the calmest of characters, to sort it out:

CHOOBUKHOV: *You'd better get married as soon as possible and – GO TO THE DEVIL! She consents!*

HE JOINS THEIR HANDS

♡ 201 ♡

> *She consents, and all the rest of it. I give you my blessing*
> *and so forth. Only leave me alone!*
> LOMOV: (Coming round) *Eh? What? Who?*
> NATALIA: *He's alive! Yes, yes, I consent!*
> LOMOV: *Eh? Who? . . . Ah! Yes, I understand . . .*
> *I'm so happy, Natalia Stepanova . . .*
> NATALIA: *I'm happy too . . . all the same, you must*
> *admit it now: Tryer is not so good a dog as Flyer.*
> LOMOV: *He's better!*
> NATALIA: *He's worse!*
> CHOOBUKHOV: *There! Family happiness has begun.*
> *Champagne! Bring the champagne!*

And on this happy note of communal hysteria the play
ends, a comic and realistic picture of two people who love
and hate at the same time!

But surely the world's favourite couple who cannot live
with each other, yet can't live apart, are the stars of that
all-time starry film, *Gone With The Wind*. In scene after
scene Clark Gable as Rhett Butler, never better, stalks
Scarlett O'Hara through the 'land of cavaliers and cotton
called the Old South' where, 'in this pretty world, gallantry
took its last bow'. Their romance is truly 'a dream
remembered', the kind of dream movie-goers have been
happy to keep on dreaming ever since the film first came
out.

For Scarlett is a flighty Southern belle, and Rhett, as he
keeps insisting, is 'not a marrying man'. What's more, she
is carrying a torch for Ashley Wilkes (stunningly languid
and lovely in Leslie Howard's performance) and because
she can't have Ashley she marries two other fellas. At last
Rhett catches up with her after the death of the second.
The grieving widow receives him with a less-than-warm
welcome:

SCARLETT: *You really are the most ill-bred man to come here at a time like this.*

RHETT: *I'll say what I came to say and then get out. I can't go on any longer without you . . . I made up my mind you were the only woman for me the first time I ever saw you at Twelve Oaks . . . So I see I shall have to marry you.*

SCARLETT: *I never heard of such bad taste!*

RHETT: *Would you be more convinced if I fell to my knees?*

SCARLETT: *Turn me loose, you varmint, and get out of here!*

Even the sweet-talking Rhett Butler is going to have his work cut out to win Scarlett. He begins by falling back on his Deep South gallantry, in a parody proposal sending up all the high-falutin' conventions that Scarlett likes to think she lives by:

RHETT: *Forgive me for startling you with the impetuosity of my sentiments, my dear Scarlett, I mean my dear Mrs Kennedy, but it cannot have escaped your notice that for some time past the friendship I have felt for you has ripened into a deeper feeling, a feeling more beautiful, more pure, more sacred, dare I name it, can it be love?*

But this elegant fooling is only the cover for his real passion. He sweeps Scarlett into his arms for a tremendous kiss:

SCARLETT: *Don't, I shall faint.*

RHETT: *I want you to faint! This is what you were meant for! None of the fools you've ever known before have kissed you like this, have they? Say you're going to marry me! Say yes! SAY YES!*

SCARLETT: *Yes!*

Oh yes, yes, yes! And fiddle-dee-dee and great balls of fire! Scarlett is still herself enough to demand a diamond ring from her betrothed, adding, 'And do buy a **GREAT BIG ONE, Rhett.'** But with all her faults, we know that he really loves her — and when he says at the end, 'Frankly, Scarlett, I don't give a damn', whoever believes that they are really finished?

Scarlett marries one of her husbands purely for his money, and is honest enough to admit that it is at least part of Rhett's attraction for her. The very reverse of this situation is true for Dorothea, the heroine of George Eliot's epic novel, *Middlemarch*. Dorothea is imprisoned by the fortune that her first husband has left her — on condition that she does not after his death marry the one man whom he knows she loves.

As a man of honour, her lover feels that he cannot ask her to forsake her wealth, and share his humble poverty. He decides to leave, and comes to her for a last goodbye:

'. . . *since I must go away — since we must always be divided — you may think of me as one on the brink of the grave.'*

While he was speaking there came a vivid flash of lightning which lit each of them up for the other — and the light seemed to be the terror of a hopeless love . . . Her lips trembled and so did his . . . they kissed tremblingly, and then they moved apart . . .

'You may see beyond the misery of it, but I don't,' said Will angrily . . . 'We shall never be married.'

'Some time — we might,' said Dorothea, in a trembling voice.

'When?' said Will bitterly. 'I could not offer myself to any woman, even if she had no luxuries to renounce.'

Will is almost determined to fling their love away. Pulled between pride and passion, he is tearing them apart. Dorothea has to try to save both him and herself:

> *At last he turned, and stretching out his hand automatically towards his hat, said with a sort of exasperation, 'Goodbye.'*
>
> *'Oh, I cannot bear it — my heart will break!' said Dorothea, starting from her seat, the flood of her young passion bearing down all the obstructions which had kept her silent — the great tears rising and falling in an instant: 'I don't mind about poverty — I hate my wealth.'*
>
> *In an instant Will was close to her and had his arms round her, but she drew her head back and held his away gently that she might go on speaking, her large, tear-filled eyes looking at his very simply while she said in a sobbing, child-like way, 'We could live quite well on my own fortune — it is too much — seven hundred a year — I want so little — no new clothes — and I will learn what everything costs.'*

Dorothea may have no idea about the cost of things, but she knows how to value true worth in her lover. From this moment the reader has no fears about the future happiness of the young couple.

As this shows, nothing is more sublime for a woman than the proposal she gets from the man she wants. All it takes is true love, and a sense of the occasion. For this reason lovers often choose St Valentine's Day to make their offer, in the knowledge that on this day of days, the god of love and all his patron saints are on their side.

One hand-made card of the Victorian period shows a church with its windows and arches all made out of lace paper. Inside, hand-written, is the simple proposal 'For dear Annie, with M.J.'s love':

Modest Proposals

If you love me
As I love you
Nothing but death
Shall part us two.

In the early days of Valentines, all these lovely things were handmade. In the absence of mass manufacture, with saccharine sweet nothings churned out in their thousands, lovers lovingly created their own from an enchanting array of lace and silver paper, forget-me-nots, roses and violets, satin, velvet and sachets of perfume. Many survive today, though fragile, still beautiful.

But sometimes to write even the simple question 'Will you be mine?' was not so easy as that. Before the 1870s most of the children of the poor never went to school. So it was a desperate struggle for them to read or write at all, and many never learned. An anonymous valentine proposal of Victorian times is a touching reminder of the lives of ordinary people in these bad old days. Hand-written, it obviously cost a tremendous effort of love, and strikingly illustrates the power of the human heart to find expression in spite of all:

My dear i rite you
just a line and
wish you a happy
valentine though
valentine is over
do not say i am
to late for if you
do i am afaered
my heart will
nearly break
Take this and read
it and except it from

The Real Thing

me it came from
the one that love the
i love the wilt
thou love me
i wonder wich love best for
your love i can
not spell so
you must guse
the rest but
if you will be
mine i will
be thine and
so good morrow
valentine

The fate of this sweet and heart-rending epistle is not known. Let's hope that his Valentine went scampering round the second she got this, to snap him up before anyone else did!

Such love is never really, as the song says, 'wasted on the young'. But it isn't their sole monopoly either. One of the greatest romances of all time involved a man who initially drew back because of his age, feeling that it separated him from the one woman he had ever truly loved. But he took the decision to 'play it, Sam' — and gave the world Bogart and Bacall.

The age-gap between them was the least of the problems that the couple had to face. As movie stars they lived in the constant glare of hostile publicity, waking up to headlines screaming:

BOGART DISCLOSES PLAN TO MARRY
BACALL, ACTOR SAYS HIS WIFE HAS
AGREED TO GIVE HIM DIVORCE

When this one was sprung on Bacall, with her amazing presence of mind in the face of the press, she quipped, 'That's the first I've heard of any engagement — he'll have to ask me first!'

And as soon as he could, Bogart did. 'Meet me in Chicago,' was his offer. 'I've got a job to do there. Then we'll go on to Louis Bromfield's farm and get married. Might as well kill two birds with one stone.' This unromantic pose was devised to throw the press off the scent, for they were still taunting him for having answered the *'BACALL OF THE WILD'*. In her autobiography Bacall gave a deep and honest insight into the way that love came into both their lives and changed all the days and nights to come:

> *How in hell can you handle love without turning your life upside down? That's what love does, it changes everything. Life would never be the same again.*

In private, Bogart was an ardent, tender, head-over-heels lover. He was ready to commit himself to the full, to give his love and never to count the cost. Bacall knew how wonderful this was:

> *Never in my life had or has a man cared so much for me, wanted so much to protect me, surround me with life's joys, share everything. It made me want to return the care — to show him it was possible to be really happy with a woman, to give him children. I was determined to do this.*

When the moment came, Bogart proposed to Bacall in the same unique and individual way that he had done everything else in his life. At the time Cole Porter's song, *Don't Fence Me In* was top of the American hit parade. Bogart wired Bacall:

PLEASE FENCE ME IN BABY THE WORLD'S TOO BIG OUT HERE AND I DON'T LIKE IT WITHOUT YOU

They married, and Bacall fulfilled all her hopes of the marriage, happiness, children, everything. As for Bogart, he found a kind of love that he had never known before. In Bacall's own words:

No one has ever written a romance better than we lived it.

Bogart and Bacall had the advantages of being rich and famous. But everyone can be a star of their own marriage moment. The perfect romance is the one between you and the person you love, and when you find your home in the heart of your own true love, nothing else matters.

Over the centuries men and women have found a thousand ways to give and to accept the greatest gift of love. These marriage proposals encapsulate the whole range of human experience. Every one is an important human drama, an everyday miracle like the mystery of life itself. Every one reflects, at that moment, the highest hope that two people have for each other, and for themselves.

Today, people sometimes hold back from getting married, when they can be together in love without it. But there is more inside marriage than outside it, more closeness, more commitment, more love. To deny this is to miss out on a kind of fulfilment not to be found anywhere else. Getting married is life's greatest adventure, and in these proposals we are privileged to share the magical moment when two lovers join their hands and hearts and embark upon it – together.